MIKE H SER'S

SCRAT MIC HIRAGANA

PLUS E CONVERSATION)

1990
THE HOKUSEIDO PRESS
Tokyo

Acknowledgements

Your author expresses his heartfelt thanks to these persons for their invaluable help and advice during the preparation of this manuscript : his colleague, Professor Yasuo Kubota of Tsuru University near the base of Mt. Fuji ; Nicky Sekino of Yokohama ; Californian Marina Lavagnino for her assistance in applying the finishing touches ; and finally to the thousands of users of this book around the world, whom he hopes will send in their suggestions to him at P.O. Box 139, Shinjuku-ku, Tokyo 163-91 to enhance its usability.

Cover design

The cover design is an original concept of the author and developed with the author's guidance, by Mr. Hajime Kobayashi of EMI Record Company of Tokyo.

Illustrations And Hiragana Ideograms

The various illustrations dispersed throughout the book were drawn by Kazuhito Murata, and Kentaro Haji.

First Edition July 1990

PRINTED IN JAPAN

THE HOKUSEIDO PRESS

Published by The Hokuseido Press
3-32-4, Honkomagome, Bunkyo-ku, Tokyo

Dedicated to my late brothers Robert and Earl, my niece Mrs. Sherrie Boyd and her future tennis champion princess / daughter Mary Elizabeth in Garland, Texas, my favorite New York cousin Mrs. Inez Atkinson and her family, my sisters Beverly and Esther, and all their children, and to all my cousins in Cleveland, Ohio and in Buffalo, New York.

Reference Hiragana/Katakana Chart

A ア	あ	I イ	い	U ウ	う	E エ	え	O オ	お
KA カ	か	KI キ	き	KU ク	く	KE ケ	け	KO コ	こ
SA サ	さ	SHI シ	し	SU ス	す	SE セ	せ	SO ソ	そ
TA タ	た	CHI チ	ち	TSU ツ	つ	TE テ	て	TO ト	と
NA ナ	な	NI ニ	に	NU ヌ	ぬ	NE ネ	ね	NO ノ	の
HA ハ	は	HI ヒ	ひ	HU FU フ	ふ	HE ヘ	へ	HO ホ	ほ
MA マ	ま	MI ミ	み	MU ム	む	ME メ	め	MO モ	も
YA ヤ	や			YU ユ	ゆ			YO ヨ	よ
RA ラ	ら	RI リ	り	RU ル	る	RE レ	れ	RO ロ	ろ
WA ワ	わ	O ヲ	を	UN ン	ん				

Mokuji : Contents

Mokuji : Contents

Mokuji : Contents

Mokuji : Contents

X

Foreword

The Hiragana Times of Shinjuku Ward in Tokyo describes SCRATCH N' MIMIC HIRAGANA PLUS JAPANESE CONVERSATION as a 'dream festival of Japanese learning'.

We, the colleagues of the author concur and take great pleasure in endorsing SCRATCH N' MIMIC HIRAGANA PLUS JAPANESE CONVERSATION. This most helpful and timely 'language student's friend' is a 'must have' book for potential users of all ages and proficiency levels interested in studying Japanese privately or in group classes.

Quite novel in design, contents and usefulness, this book makes learning fun, despite the complications of Japanese. Picking up where other self-teaching books fall short, the near-frustrated student of hiragana finds SCRATCH N' MIMIC HIRAGANA PLUS JAPANESE CONVERSATION is truly a 'dream festival of learning' rich with opportunities for the easy comprehension of the Japanese language. The variety of learning stimuli ensure smooth acquisition of the lessons if not by one explanation then by others.

The author's great advantage in compiling this book results in part from his more than a decade of residency in Japan. The insight of this valuable book can only come from an author who has study experiences at two famous Japanese universities as well as at New York's Columbia University. The timeliness of this book is a by-product of the author's constant search for ways to make learning Japanese as easy as possible.

The author, well aware of the constant changes and continuing hardships from his personal living experiences and from learning Japanese firsthand, here offers counsel and guidance in a supportive and light hearted manner, which in part are his credentials for putting this book together.

Why do lucky users of SCRATCH N' MIMIC HIRAGANA PLUS JAPANESE CONVERSATION discover it to be the most helpful text available to anyone wishing for basic Japanese reading, writing and speaking dexterity? Because of :

* There are over 100 delightfully humorous cut-out and carry-around Hiragana cards. Hiragana sounds are illustrated with real-life situations which help associate the caricature action with a particular ideogram (letter) to be learned which always appears in the upper right corner. Its use in a Hiragana word appears directly below. This affords the learner a chance to

immediately recognize, remember and understand the ideogram to be practiced in writing. This easy-to-follow formula draws the learner into the text, while providing vocabulary, visual impact and pure learning pleasure. With a little imagination they can also be used as playing cards while studying Japanese (Nihongo).

* Its essential detailed and informative grammar explanations presented in a clear way and provide examples. These help to build a solid foundation for a smooth and easy transition into more serious study of the Japanese language.
* This learning-by-doing book has an easy-to-use format which focuses on forming cursive strokes, reproducing accurate kana models, pronunciation, common mistakes and augmenting vocabulary.
* Each chapter is packed with creative and stimulating activities like word games, quizzes, and crossword puzzles so that with a Japanese study-mate each can share the other's culture for mutual understanding. These activities add a sparkle of fun to the learning process.
* This well organized easy-to-use "learning-by-doing" book easily integrates with any Japanese curriculum and is ideal for classroom courses, and independent or tutorial study as it is a big enough book for share-reading.
* Its categorized, Romanized grammar related conversation phrases with bracketed letters indicating the degree of politeness.

We feel confident you will agree that popular SCRATCH N' MIMIC HIRAGANA PLUS JAPANESE CONVERSATION earns a 10-star rating for presenting an exciting new approach to tackling the study of Japanese.

Authors : Yasuo Kubota
Tsuru Bunka University, Yamanashi, and
Dr. Chuichi I. Sasaki of Tokyo

Fun With Hiragana Combinations

DOODLE

AS ON OTHER PAGES, THESE MOSTLY MEANINGLESS COMBINATIONS OF SOUNDS WHOSE LETTERS ARE DRAWN SO THAT THEY RESEMBLE HUMAN FACES. THEY PROVIDE YOU A GOOD ARMCHAIR HOBBY MIMICKING WRITING KANA IDEOGRAMS FOR PRACTICE PURPOSES.

へへへは

Poetic giggling expression

はにわ

An ancient clay figure

ひひひさこ

Hisako, a female name

さけダメダメヨ

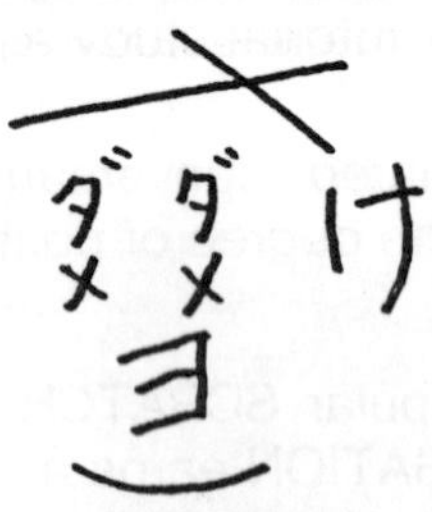

I can't drink rice wine

すすきのほ

Pulp of a wild weed

つる二八〇〇ムし

Phone number Tsuru 280-064

つつうらうら

Everywhere

へのへのもへじ

(this has no meaning)

へのへのもじ

The letters HENO HENO

1 This Kana Book Layout

As the title implies, **SCRATCH N' MIMIC HIRAGANA Plus JAPANESE CONVERSATION** is primarily intended to pass on 'know how' hints to readers interested in not only speaking Japanese as a second language, but equally instructs how to properly write and read **hiragana**, (the cursive simplified written form of the difficult Japanese logograms known as **kanji**,) from scratch.

Towards achieving this aim, prior to the start of writing **kana** (**hiragana** and **katakana**) an illustrated **kana** familiarization page contains the five (later reduced to three) main kana to be learned. Each illustrated cut-out card which can be carried around for study purposes, contains a related **hiragana** ideogram, a Romanized hiragana word and its approximate English translation. The illustrated cards serve as a memory warm-up and vocabulary expander. After the reader has understood how each **kana** looks and is written, he is in a better position to also try to learn how to pronounce what he has seen.

At the top of each page is a whole **kana**. A style recognition box at the left side displays the last **kana** stroke written, a middle box contains the current **kana** to be written, and the right side box indicates the next kana to be practiced.

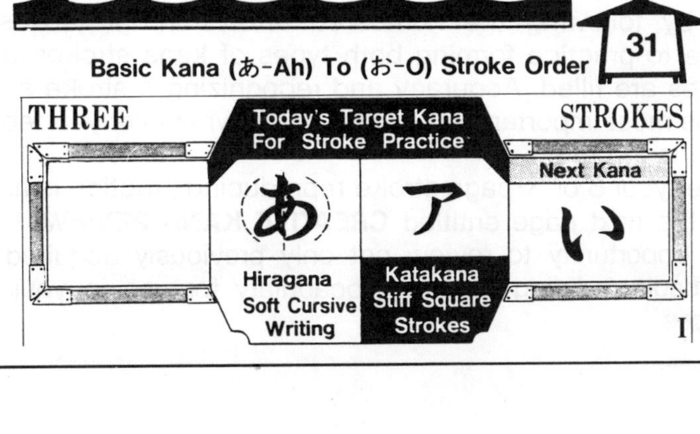

2 This Kana Book Layout

Immediately below, the two main middle boxes, containing **hiragana** and **katakana** side by side, has been placed in a broad instruction box (**HINTS FOR STROKE ORDER REPRODUCTION AND RECOGNITION**) bearing hints on how that particular **kana** is pronounced and other pertinent information.

Hints For Stroke Order Reproduction And Recognition

(あ-**ah**) is the pronunciation for this kana. It is roughly pronounced like the '**ah**' in father but don't open your mouth as wide. Avoid Kana Similarity Problems. Although the top stroke is the same for the kana (あ-**a**) and (ま-**ma**), notice the next two strokes for both kana. Beware of the loops. Be sure to write each kana accurately less one be mistaken for the other.

Then, below that box are the **kana** stroke reproduction boxes. They contain a model of the main **kana** to be practiced in the 'target stroke' box at the extreme left. The number of strokes

Model of main Kana →

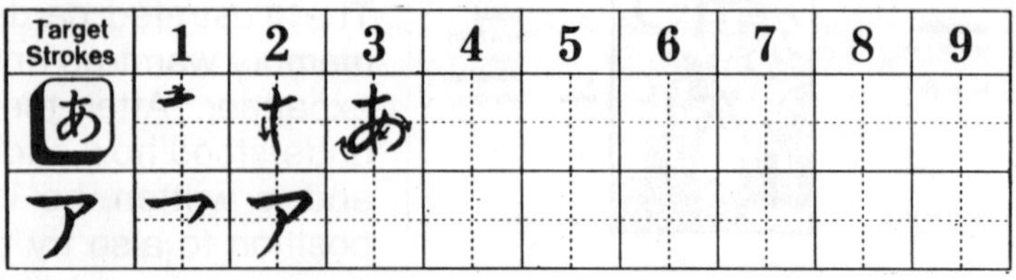

required to write the model **kana** are indicated by the tiny numbers in the stroke reproduction boxes, as well as by the bold numbers which appear above the boxes. The easiest part of all is that you can learn how to scratch (write) **kana** correctly, on your own, merely by following the numbered arrows in the boxes. You continue to practice forming both types of **kana** strokes until all the boxes are filled. Accuracy and recognizing a stroke size, not speed, is most important. Use extra paper whenever you feel more practice is in order.

After your 5 or 3-page stroke reproducing practice is finished, turn to the next page entitled **CREATIVE KANA REVIEW.** It offers you an opportunity to review not only previously acquired kana, but to begin building up new vocabulary for use in your future sentences.

This Kana Book Layout 3

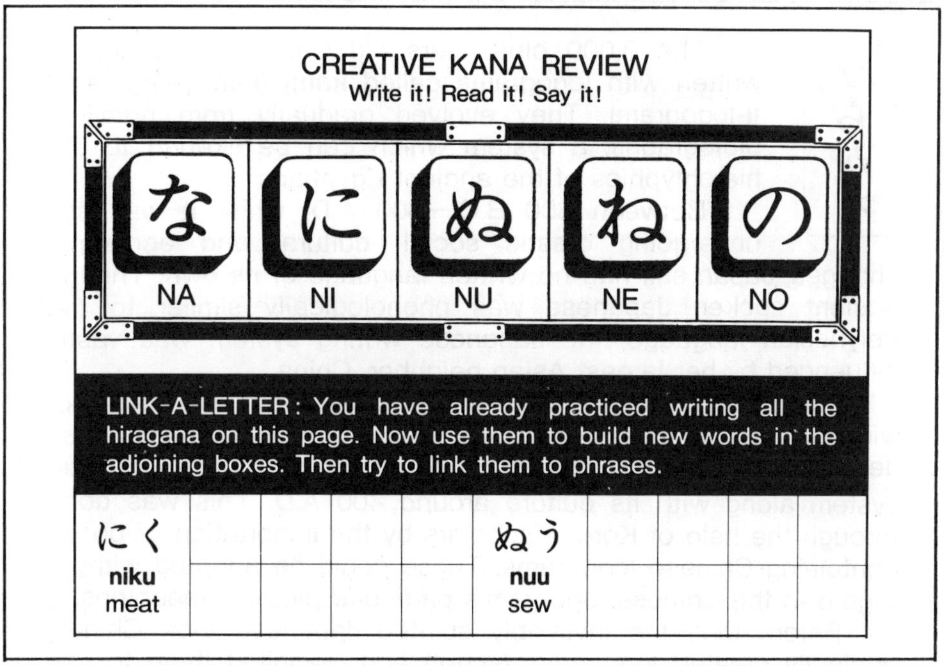

Twist Your Tongue With These Tongue Twisters

It would be helpful to you if you practiced with a Japanese friend saying these tongue twisters several times a day to keep from tripping over Japanese words you are trying to pronounce. Also you'll find it fun if you inject them into some of your conversation. Let's go !

1) **Akamaki-gami, kimaki-gami, aomaki-gami chamaki-gami.**
The red paper, the yellow paper, the blue paper and the brown paper.

2) **Ano nageshi no naganaginata wa taga naganaginata zo !**
Whose long sword is marked "nageshi"?

4 How Kana For Writing Japanese Originated

ひらがな

The 3,000 plus years old Chinese language is written with logograms called **kanji** (**kan**-China, and, **ji**-logogram). They evolved gradually from primitive pictographs, a system which can be likened to the hieroglyphics of the ancient Egyptians.

Between 300 B.C.—300 A.D. while it was still undergoing drastic social, cultural and economic changes, Japan still had no written language of its own. Though ancient spoken Japanese was phonologically similar to the Polynesian language, the Japanese writing system was vastly influenced by her largest Asian neighbor, China.

Being the 'borrowers' they still are, when the Japanese got wind of the fact that China possessed a written language, they decided that they 'just had to borrow' some of China's linguistic system along with its culture around 400 A.D. This was done through the help of Korean scholars by the importation of books containing Chinese logograms. These could be adopted without regard to the Chinese logogram's particular pictorial meanings.

Before long the invincibly spirited Japanese took China's originally created logograms (script) and reapplied them to raw spoken Japanese words of a simple nature called '**manyogana.**' Through refinement by matching many Chinese script to their own, the Japanese eventually developed new pronunciations for the basic meanings of Chinese script.

While it became possible to use Chinese script to write the basic kana root of words, it couldn't be used to express the Japanese grammatical structure, which differs vastly from Chinese.

After all, this language of complex script was not originally created to accommodate written Japanese. Mainly because of this and the fact that spoken Japanese bore absolutely no resemblance to spoken Chinese, and this holds true even to this very day, the majority of Japanese had extreme difficulty in understanding the non-native Chinese.

In the meantime, gradually the practice of writing Chinese script in a vertical column from top to bottom and left to right on a page became widespread among the Japanese elite class.

It took the lapse of a hundred years for the Japanese to lay the foundation of the written native Japanese language in order to make handling of the difficult Chinese script easier for the common people.

How Kana For Writing Japanese Originated 5

In the 8th century at a time known as Japan's classical age when its literature reached its zenith, on the scene appeared a Buddhist priest, Kobo Daishi (771-835). Along with other scholars he is given credit for siphoning whole segments of original Chinese script and abbreviating them into a pure, refined and simplified auxiliary Japanese phonetic-based writing syllabary (alphabet), 48 ideograms, which would enable Japanese to write grammatical endings and all the vowel and consonant sounds of the Japanese language.

They christened their relatively rounded, new, smooth and elegant cursive-shaped native phonetic syllabary, which when completed resembled very beautiful forms, manyogana (**hiragana**).

Japanization of Chinese Logogram Into Hiragana

Transformation From Kanji To Hiragana

Original kanji: **Ancient Chinese** meaning: to add		Siphoned Part		Newly Created Cursive Script Cursive Writing
				Hiragana
加	⇨	力	⇨	**Ka** か
Step 1 Basic **From this**		Step 2 Middle **To this**		Step 3 Final Script **Finally to this**

Additional Transformed Kanji/Hiragana Examples:

				Hiragana
安	⇨	あ	⇨	**Ah** あ

6 How kana For Writing Japanese Originated

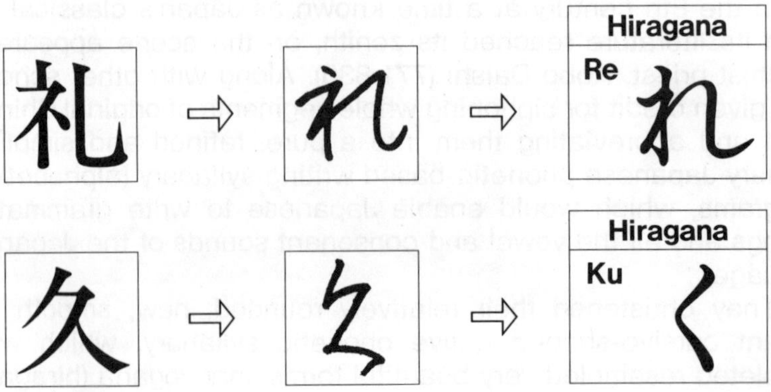

The principle purpose of the more widely used **hiragana** is for use in writing grammatical function words to 'cement' **kanji** into more precise, grammatically correct sentences. Secondary uses include the writing of particles, certain common texts, and inflectional endings. It is also used for writing Japanese words which can't be transformed into **kanji**. It's used alongside Chinese script to express their pronunciation, and to express ordinary Japanese words written in personal and business letters, books, magazines, newspapers, and for train station names along with **kanji**.

Shortly after the invention of **hiragana**, by extracting certain unchanged portions of **kanji**, some native Japanese Buddhist priests developed a second identical set of simplistic phonetic sound syllabary from **manyokana** called **katakana** (or, partial ideo grams). Distinctly squarish / angular in shape, the extended unsmooth appearance of its stiff straight line strokes causes it to effectively stand out when mixed with **kanji** and **hiragana** in Japanese writings. Compared to **kanji** and **hiragana,** it is the simplest of the three Japanese writing systems.

The primary purposes of **katakana** are to serve as a reminder of how Chinese words were to be pronounced in Japanese, and to phonetically transcribe thousands of foreign words, called 'loan words' including personal names, place names, products, animals, plants, telegrams, names of foreigners, advertisements, and diseases.

By the 9th century all three writing systems were in use. Function-wise, the role of **kanji** was to form the basic building blocks which represented a sentence's principal ideas, actions or objects, while **kana** completed the picture with particles, prepositions and verb modifiers.

How Kana For Writing Japanese Originated 7

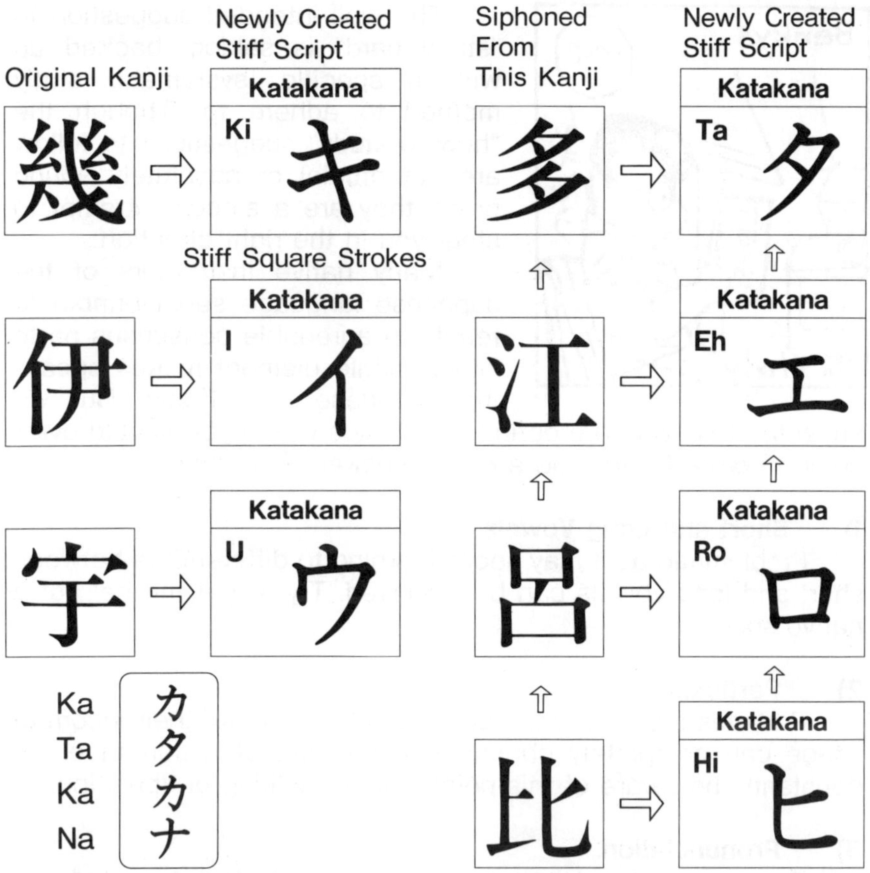

Japanese is linguistically unique, in that it presents a great difference in the languages used by men and women. Also there is both a masculine and a feminine system of pronunciation which dates back to the Heian Era. Katakana was referred to as men's script (**otoko moji**), since Chinese loan words were generally used only by men. In ancient times, conversing as they do now, men normally used such blunt terms as **da na, sa, yo,** and **ya** at the end of their conversation. These are only a few examples of male expressions.

The female language even to this day is usually spoken with the honorific **'o'**. Thus most of their expressions will end with the last word being pronounced as either **ne, na no, na no yo, wa, da wa, wa yo,** or simply **no**.

8 How To Overcome Second Language Learning Obstacles Easily

The well-intended suggestion to "study hard" is seldom backed up with a specific, systematic study method to adhere to. Though the "how to study" suggestions to follow are not official or absolutely sound proof, they are a sincere attempt to steer you in the right direction.

Many native instructors of the Japanese language seem unable to reach an agreeable consensus as to which single element makes speaking Japanese so difficult. But we know the following are definite obstacles which you should overcome in order to become a good speaker of Japanese.

1) Short and Long Vowels

Problematic as it may seem, learning to differentiate between short and long vowels can be achieved. Try to get the help of a native speaker.

2) Particles

Particles are only small connecting words, but their incorrect usage can completely change the meaning of a sentence. So constantly be aware of this point whether writing or speaking.

3) Pronunciation

Because many Japanese words are similar in sound but entirely different in meaning, this can make the learning process a more serious problem than the placement of particles in a sentence. If you are trying to get across a point with a mispronounced word, you will give a completely distorted meaning. So be extra careful.

4) Formality In Speech

Equally troublesome is learning to use the different levels of formality in speech. To help eliminate this pesty problem to some degree, your author has bracketed Romanized Japanese conversation sentences included in this book with either (*vp*-very polite), (*p*-polite), (*o*-ordinary), (*s*-slang), (*c*)-colloquial, (*e*-spoken by everybody), (*m*-spoken by man) and (*f*-spoken by females).

How To Overcome Second Language Learning Obstacles Easily

9

The easiest way to overcome these obstacles would be to acquire a strong basic foundation of the Japanese language, build a strong general vocabulary and then eventually focus on a specialized area of study geared to your specific interests. Rest assured that besides motivating you, this will enable you to better accomplish your goals. Also, as memorization and drills are a most essential language learning tool, be aware that there is no magic formula for getting around this. Furthermore, if you decide on a strict self-study program, strict self-discipline is of the utmost importance. Then, Japanese won't be so hard to learn.

Finally, as frustrating as misused words, strange sentences without particles and literal translations making no sense may be, using the Japanese language outside one's study place, while transacting business or when socializing with Japanese acquaintances is the most effective and rewarding as well as least tiresome way to get to speak Japanese.

Systematic Self Or Group Study Basic Steps

Prior to learning your written **hiragana a**(あ), **i**(い), **u**(う), **e**(え), **o**(お) alphabet, it's best to start off with Romanized letters as a basic foundation and gradually work your way up to **kana**. If you have no systematic way of studying on your own, you may just find the following suggestions helpful for learning conventional daily Japanese exchange phrases and sentences for eventual future use.

1) If there are no qualified private tutors or community centers in your area offering evening Japanese language study programs, you have another choice. Look for an opportunity to become acquainted with Japanese in your's or a nearby community. Since they may have the same objectives as you ; getting to know each other's language, culture, community or country through mutual help, you're on your way to learning Japanese.

With the full understanding that, just by virtue of being a native Japanese speaker doesn't necessarily qualify them as a language instructor, ask them to help you learn Japanese. They may have the desire, readiness and willingness to help you, but not the faintest idea of how to go about it. You'll have to plan your study strategy in advance and talk it over with them.

2) The kind of study supervision you will want your new language helpmate to provide, will be to catch any reading, writing, and speaking mistakes needing correction.

3) Learn to speak and write complete sentence construction patterns, and phrases in short or long paragraphs, but not in chopped-up sentences. And make doubly sure that what you are saying makes sense. Repeat over and over troublesome words, phrases, and responses until your helpmate feels that they are understandable and sound natural to native Japanese ears.

4) For accuracy, always carefully review your textbook or self-made Romanized Japanese or **hiragana** dialog sentences, phrases and words before going on to a new lesson page. Cover the English sentences and say aloud the Japanese equivalent for memorization's sake. You'll be increasing your much needed vocabulary. Of course, feel free to look at any words covered that either you or your helpmate feel are mispronounced. During the process don't forget to practice the responses, too. Make paper tests so your helpmate can check on your progress.

Take your studying a step further by exchanging cassette tapes and letters with a language exchange penpal who is willing to review your spoken and written Japanese. You can do the same for that language exchange penpal.

5) A Romanized Japanese-English dictionary can be an indispensable tool when you come across words that have more than one meaning. Let your helpmate, or any Japanese you can approach, assist you in deciding on a properly suitable word for that particular situation in which you intend to use it.

6) If you are a resident or short-time visitor in Japan, the more words and phrases you know for daily social amenities, the happier will be your existence. Speak **bluffer's Japanese** with confidence. Don't fear making mistakes. That's a defeatist attitude. All languages are difficult to learn, not just Japanese. But none are impossible.

7) In order to increase your vocabulary, whenever possible, always carry around a small notebook with a list of Japanese words and phrases categorized by specific titles into separate sections. Have your language on the left page and Japanese on the right page. Be sure to always add new words to what you already have and use them without hesitation.

8) Employ a Japanese-acquisition saturation method by simply observing **kana** ads connected with public transportation, tv programs, menus, magazines and newspapers, cinemas, and stores. Eavesdrop on Japanese conversation in a discreet way, talk with Japanese on a daily basis as much as possible. Try to live with Japanese, attend public events, and if lady luck is so kind, marry a Japanese. In such an event try to dispense with dictionaries as quickly as possible.

9) In your quest to learn Japanese, don't go overboard becoming native by breaking off contact with speakers of your mother tongue. There'll be times when you'll need their warmth, psychological support, and friendship. Learn their secrets from them, if they have any, of successfully studying Japanese.

10) Should you decide to formally study Japanese, visit a language school for study ideas, on the pretense you may possibly enroll in a few courses. Don't study at a school that programs a heavy demanding study schedule.

11) For a bit of relaxing study, without looking at your textbook, gradually listen to replays of dialog words, phrases and sentences previously recorded by your study helpmate. Turn off the cassette tape and repeat aloud what you just have heard. Every time your helpmate expresses dissatisfaction, continue the rewinding and pronunciation process. Repetition is a learning key.

12) If you don't continue to make too many noticeable mistakes, then you are ready to start your real live Japanese conversation. Eventually you'll be able to express yourself in Japanese naturally.

13) There's no particular best time of the day or night to study. It all depends on your daily schedule, physical condition, frame of mind and mood. But always study in a relaxed atmosphere with no disturbing elements around or pressing business left unfinished.

12 Basic First Steps To Writing Kana Ideograms

There is no mystery to writing the soft cursive flowing syllabric **hiragana** ideograms. In order to begin forming cursive **kana** strokes first get accustomed to being systematic. Rules must be observed in order to accurately form hiragana ideograms of varying sizes and forms easily recognizeable to the eyes of native Japanese. So take just a few minutes to go over these suggested simple **kana** writing rules.

Proper Kana Stroke Writing Sequence

Whenever you are about to write any **kana** ideograms or want to Japanicize words from your mother tongue, try to get a native Japanese to help you in person or by mail. He'll initially draw as near perfect as possible a few **hiragana** and later **katakana** model brush or pen strokes. It is important to memorize by sight the proper traditionally accepted starting order of each individually written **kana** ideogram. Do your best in redrawing them while simultaneously getting a feeling for stroking. Repeat the exercise until you feel satisfied that your strokes resemble the original ones you're trying to imitate. Frankly speaking, it's more difficult to convert Japanese words into foreign languages than the reverse. But we're sure you can make it a joy. Happy efforts !

Horizontal Style

きって

postage stamp

Keep in mind that there are two Japanese writing forms. The horizontal writing form whose stroke writing sequence always starts from the upper left side of a sheet of paper and ends in the lower right section in the same style as Western written matters.

Vertical Style

きって

postage stamp

Vertically written matter is always started from the upper top right side of a sheet of paper and ends at the lower left bottom section of the paper. Whether Japanese should be written horizontally or vertically is the writer's decision alone to make. Decide which style pleases you and suits your particular purpose since both styles are perfectly acceptable in Japan. Normally, matters concerning the natural science field are written horizontally and matters concerning literature are written vertically, but this is not a steadfast rule.

Incidentally, Japanese normally open kanji books from their right side whereas most other people open books from their left side. Thus, 'Japanese open their books at the point where we close ours'.

Three Ways To Finish Writing A Stroke

1) The three accepted ways to bring your stroke-writing to a final punctuated end are referred to as **tome**, **hane**, and **harai**.

a) The meaning of the word **'tome'** (stop) is a clear indication that at the last finishing stroke of a **hiragana** ideogram you slide it into a glide upward, while at the same time lifting your writing instrument right off the paper. Placing a period next to a **kana** ideogram immediately after that action places it in a **tome** (stop) category.

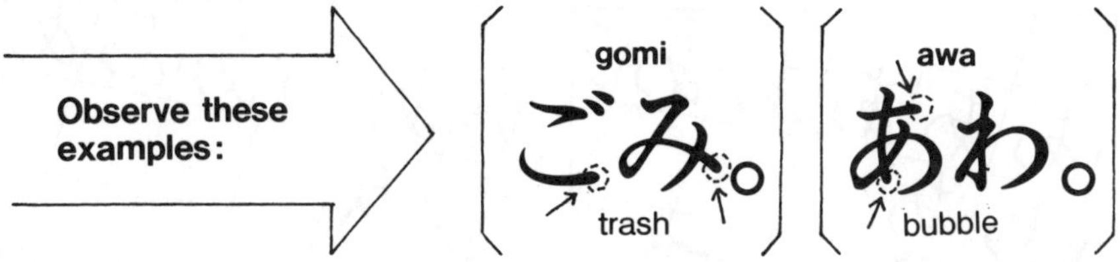

b) **Hane** (jump) is the second method of ending the writing of a **hiragana** stroke. The ending is achieved by adding a reflex tail to the final stroke, circled with an arrow pointed at it in the following examples.

Basic First Steps To Writing Kana Ideograms

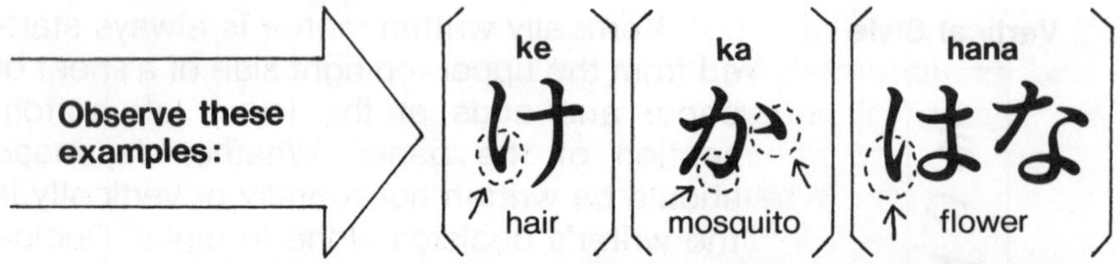

c) The third method of ending your stroke writing sequence is brought about by the use of **harai** (sweeping). To end with a pretty stroke is not as simple as it may seem, thus a lot of practice is called for. Midway towards ending your final written stroke gradually, but gently, in a feather motion-like glide lift your writing instrument from the paper. In the process leave a faint fading trail. Get an idea of the technique from these examples.

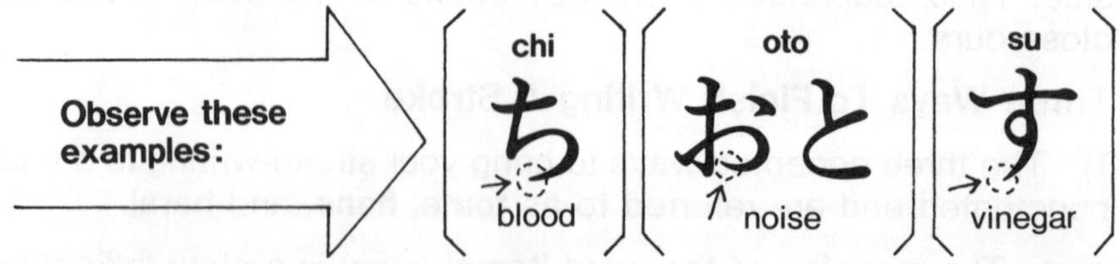

In cases like these, where the stroke of a hiragana ideogram lacks an ending indicator, depending on their place in a sentence, either **hane** (jump) or **tome** (stop) endings will be used. And speaking of endings, this ends our little orientation on the first steps to writing hiragana strokes.

Write Your Hiragana Strokes Legibly

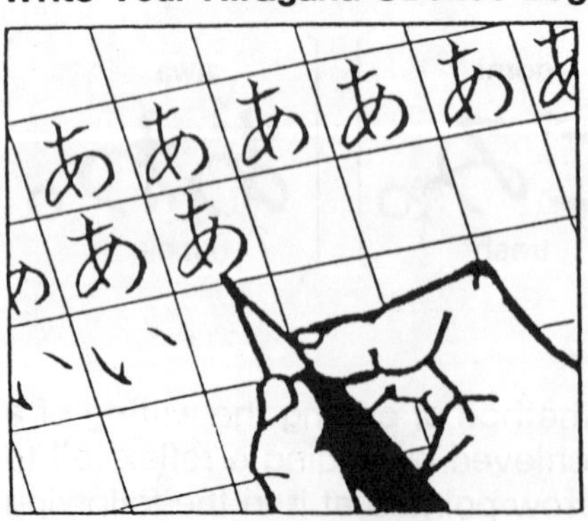

Correctly written

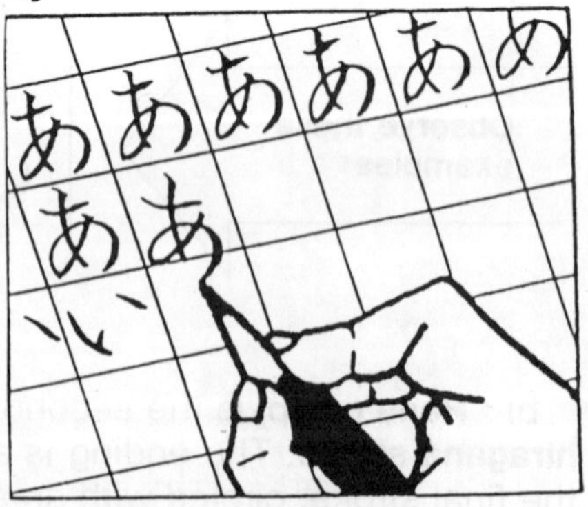

Incorrectly written

Basic First Steps To Writing Kana Ideograms 15

The left illustration shows a properly written stroke. Notice how this accurately written stroke correctly fills the square.

The right illustration shows a poorly written stroke. Notice how the square into which the ideogram should fit was ignored. Don't let this happen. Whether copying a stroke or writing on your own, always imitate the left illustrated model.

From here on it, you will begin writing both **hiragana** and **katakana** strokes which appear on the same practice page in stroke boxes. Be sure to draw horizontal and vertical **kana** strokes accurately and to keep proper spacing between strokes in sentences. Improperly drawn strokes can cause one **kana** word to be mistaken for another.

A Note of Caution:

These are **hiragana** ideograms which, because they look alike, can be quite confusing at times. Be sure to make yourself aware of their difference in appearance.

1)	あ	A	☞	お	O	7)	ね	NE	☞	ぬ	NU
2)	い	I	☞	こ	KO	8)	は	HA	☞	ほ	HO
3)	う	U	☞	ら	RA	9)	ま	MA	☞	も	MO
4)	さ	SA	☞	き	KI	10)	め	ME	☞	ぬ	NU
5)	さ	SA	☞	ち	CHI	11)	る	RU	☞	ろ	RO
6)	な	NA	☞	た	TA	12)	わ	WA	☞	れ	RE

Mistakes often occur in the writing of these ideograms. Be sure not to write them incorrectly. All the ideograms on the left and right side of each column are in correct form.

Basic First Steps To Writing Kana Ideograms

wrong		correct		wrong		correct	
カ	for	か	KA	さ	for	ち	CHI
〉	for	く	KU	ほ	for	ほ	HO
J	for	し	SHI	ま	for	ま	MA

A Word On Japanese Punctuation Marks

When writing Japanese sentences, this mark (、) is comparable to the English comma while this mark (。) is equivalent to the period in English sentences. This mark (「　」) is used as quotation marks for horizontally written or typed sentences whereas this mark (﹂) is used for vertically written or typed sentences.

Observe the following example sentences.

かれのやくそくは、あてにならない。
Kare no yakusoku wa, ate ni naranai.
His promises aren't to be relied on.

「わたしは、あんぜんなところをさがしているぼうめいしゃです。」
Watashi wa, anzen na tokoro o sagashite iru bōmeisha desu.
"I'm a defector seeking political asylum."

「ぼうめいのきょかをとれるようにたすけてあげます。」
Bōmei no kyoka o toreru yō ni tasukete agemasu.
"We'll help you to get political asylum."

Japanese Hiragana Syllabary Sounds Chart

1. 46 Basic Hiragana

VOWELS		CONSONANTS									
	⬇	K	S	T	N	H	M	Y	R	W	N
あ a	➡	か ka	さ sa	た ta	な na	は ha	ま ma	や ya	ら ra	わ wa	ん n
い i	➡	き ki	し shi	ち chi	に ni	ひ hi	み mi		り ri		
う u	➡	く ku	す su	つ tsu	ぬ nu	ふ fu	む mu	ゆ yu	る ru		
え e	➡	け ke	せ se	て te	ね ne	へ he	め me		れ re		
お o	➡	こ ko	そ so	と to	の no	ほ ho	も mo	よ yo	ろ ro	を o	

2. 20 Dakuon and 5 Handakuon

が ga	ざ za	だ da	ば ba	ぱ pa
ぎ gi	じ ji	ぢ ji	び bi	ぴ pi
ぐ gu	ず zu	づ zu	ぶ bu	ぷ pu
げ ge	ぜ ze	で de	べ be	ぺ pe
ご go	ぞ zo	ど do	ぼ bo	ぽ po

3. 36 Yo-on

21 Basic Yōon							12 Voiced/3 Semi-voiced				
きゃ kya	しゃ sha	ちゃ cha	にゃ nya	ひゃ hya	みゃ mya	りゃ rya	ぎゃ gya	じゃ ja	ぢゃ ja	びゃ bya	ぴゃ pya
きゅ kyu	しゅ shu	ちゅ chu	にゅ nyu	ひゅ hyu	みゅ myu	りゅ ryu	ぎゅ gyu	じゅ ju	ぢゅ ju	びゅ byu	ぴゅ pyu
きょ kyo	しょ sho	ちょ cho	にょ nyo	ひょ hyo	みょ myo	りょ ryo	ぎょ gyo	じょ jo	ぢょ jo	びょ byo	ぴょ pyo

18 Tips For Converting Short Vowel Sounds Into Long Vowel Sounds

How To Pronounce Japanese

As you continue reading this rough guide to pronouncing Japanese you'll gradually become more aware that Japanese syllables can be placed in four categories : 1) five vowels (**A-(あ), I-(い), U-(う), E-(え), O-(お)**), 2) consonants plus a vowel, 3) a consonant plus a semi-vowel plus a vowel, and 4) **'UN-(ん)'**. All syllables are to be pronounced in a short crisp way with just about the same length of voice stress.

Additionally, do keep in mind that this pronunciation guide is not presented as some sort of official summary of Japanese phonetics, but merely as an aid in helping learners of Japanese to attain approximate pronunciation in the absence of a native Japanese study helpmate.

Sounds of Letters

SHORT VOWELS

These are the five Japanese vowels. They may also be syllables in themselves.

Hiragana	-a あ	-i い	-u う	-e え	-o お
Katakana	ア	イ	ウ	エ	オ
Rōmaji	"ah"	"ee"	"oo"	"eh"	"oh"
Pronounce as	'a' in America	'i' in image	'u' in hula	'e' in pet	'o' in oil

* When (**a**-あ) and (**i**-い) are paired as (**ai**-あい) to make a long vowel, neither is longer than the other.
* The vowel (**i**-い) is normally written by making it (**ii**-いい).
* The vowel (**u**-う) is pronounced as a simple vowel with unrounded lips.
* The vowel (**e**-え) in its long form is normally written as the vowel cluster (**ei**-えい) and presented as the double vowel (**ee**-ええ) which is also sometimes seen in writings.
* To express the extended (lengthened) vowel (**o**-お) in written **hiragana**, it is traditionally written as (**ō**-おお) but the generally accepted version is (**ō**-おう).

* (**o**-を) besides being pronounced as a simple vowel is also used as a particle (**o**-を) in a sentence.

"**i**" And "**u**" Vowel Sounds Are Devocalized

In places like Tokyo, and the southern part of Honshu, Japan's central island, as well as the southern island of Kyushu, if the speech isn't really spoken very slowly and carefully articulated, the vowels i and u are not devocalized. Otherwise, whenever they appear between voiceless consonants (**f, h, k, p, s, t**) or are placed at the end of a sentence, where the final syllable of a word begins with a voiceless consonant then the vowels **i** and **u** are pronounced at a low whispered pitch sound.

Notice the following examples:

desu →	**(DEsu)**	to be
shiken →	**(shi-KE-n)**	an exam
fukai →	**(fuKA-i)**	deep
chikai →	**(chiKA-i)**	near

LONG VOWELS

"What is a long vowel?" you may ask. Well, a long vowel simply means the automatic doubling of a short single vowel to an identical vowel which when pronounced is held twice as long as its original. Long vowels equal two vowels 'cemented' together.

As you'll see later, the five vowels are to be pronounced long or short depending on the word. In Romanized print, a line placed directly over a particular letter of a word (**ē**) indicates it is to be given a long sound. A short vowel can also be followed by another different vowel like: **ai-**, **ei-**, **ue-**, **and ou-** to give it a doubled sound. In katakana, to lengthen a vowel a bar is placed at the right of a vowel.

If you use the Hepburn Romanization system, which is used in this book, then you must draw a short vertical bar atop the (**ō**) to make it look like a double vowel. But in some books using the government Romanization system (**kunrei**) the **'o'** would look like this **'ou'** or **'oo'**. Whichever the case, do bear in mind that changing the duration of a vowel sound can change the meaning of a word.

20 Tips For Converting Short Vowel Sounds Into Long Vowel Sounds

Look at this chart for long and short vowel comparison

From	**To**		
Take original vowel (short)	Add to make Long vowels	Katakana	Rōmaji
a－(あ)	aa　ああ	アー	ā
i－(い)	i i　いい	イー	ii
u－(う)	uu　うう	ウー	ū
e－(え)	ee　ええ(えい)	エー	ē　ei
o－(お)	oo　おお(おう)	オー	ō　ou

Look carefully at these short and long vowels. Try to imagine the total confusion that could occur by altering the meaning of words if strict attention is not paid to the difference of pitch sound levels between short and long vowels. Look at these examples.

Short vowels		**Long vowels**	
obasan	aunt	**obāsan**	grandma
dōzo	please	**dōzō**	statue
e	picture	**ē**	yes
mo	also	**mō**	already
odori	a dance	**ōdōri**	the main street
biru	a building	**biiru**	beer
		Nyū yōku	New York
		menyū	menu

* While writing **Katakana** to express a double (**o-**ウー) vowel merely add a dash (ー) next to the (**o-**ウー) instead of an additional **Kana.**

For example: カ (**ka**) becomes カー (**kā**)

Other examples:

か (**ka**) becomes かあ (**kā**)　　き (**ki**) becomes きい (**kii**)

く (**ku**) becomes くう (**kū**)　　ね (**ne**) becomes ねえ (**nē**)

と (**to**) becomes either とう (**tō**) or とお (**tō**)

The following **kana** chart indicates which consonants may precede any of the five vowels and form syllabic sound variation combinations.

Vowel / Consonsnt	a			i			u			e			o		
	Hiragana	Katakana	Rōmaji	**Hiragana**	Katakana	Rōmaji	**Hiragana**	Katakana	Rōmaji	**Hiragana**	Katakana	Rōmaji	**Hiragana**	Katakana	Rōmaji
g	が	ガ	ga	ぎ	ギ	gi	ぐ	グ	gu	げ	ゲ	ge	ご	ゴ	go
z, j	ざ	ザ	za	じ	ジ	ji	ず	ズ	zu	ぜ	ゼ	ze	ぞ	ゾ	zo
d, j, z	だ	ダ	da	ぢ	ヂ	ji	づ	ヅ	zu	で	デ	de	ど	ド	do
b	ば	バ	ba	び	ビ	bi	ぶ	ブ	bu	べ	ベ	be	ぼ	ボ	bo

Kana sound variations are divided into these three categories.

Dakuon Sounds

Both kana syllabaries make possible the reproduction of consonated voice sounds for the voiceless consonants **(k)**, **(s)**, **(t)** and **(h)**, as well as syllables starting with the consonants **(g)**, **(z)**, **(d)** and **(b)**. In order to give voiceless sounds a counterpart, the adding of voiced sounds called **dakuon** to the voiceless consonants is accomplished with two tiny marks. One mark is two tiny parallel bars called **nigori** (゛) or, **dakuten** which are added at the upper right side of each consonant. For example (**ka**-か) becomes (**ga**-が), (**ku**- く) becomes (**gu**- ぐ) and so on. Bear in mind that although these two voiced counterparts were changed from one form to another, they still receive the same length of pronunciation.

Using Consonants And Basic Vowels

Consonant Plus Vowel Sounds

The following chart indicates which consonants may precede and form syllabic combinations with the five vowels.

22 Kana Combination Sound Changes

HIRAGANA Chart

	K	G	S	Z	T	D	N	H	B	P	M	Y	R	W	N
あ a	か ka	が ga	さ sa	ざ za	た ta	だ da	な na	は ha	ば ba	ぱ pa	ま ma	や ya	ら ra	わ wa	ん n
い i	き ki	ぎ gi	し shi	じ ji	ち chi	ぢ ji	に ni	ひ hi	び bi	ぴ pi	み mi		り ri		
う u	く ku	ぐ gu	す su	ず zu	つ tsu	づ zu	ぬ nu	ふ hu	ぶ bu	ぷ pu	む mu	ゆ yu	る ru		
え e	け ke	げ ge	せ se	ぜ ze	て te	で de	ね ne	へ he	べ be	ぺ pe	め me		れ re		
お o	こ ko	ご go	そ so	ぞ zo	と to	ど do	の no	ほ ho	ぼ bo	ぽ po	も mo	よ yo	ろ ro		

Making Voiced Sounds

A voiced sound is indicated by either the two parallel bars placed at the upper right side of a syllable (゛) or by a small circle (゜) which are called **nigori**. See these examples.

Examples :	どこ	そば	せんぷうき	きっぷ
	doko	**soba**	**senpūki**	**kippu**
	where	nearby	fan	ticket

Sound Transformation Steps

① **K with this added mark (゛) becomes g**

Ka か → Ga が

か ka → が ga
き ki → ぎ gi
く ku } becomes → ぐ gu
け ke → げ ge
こ ko → ご go

Ki き → Gi ぎ

Ku く → Gu ぐ

Ke け → Ge げ

Ko こ → Go ご

② S with this added mark (゛) becomes z

さ sa	becomes	→ ざ za
し shi		→ じ ji
す su		→ ず zu
せ se		→ ぜ ze
そ so		→ ぞ zo

Sa さ Za ざ　Shi し Ji じ
Su す Zu ず　Se せ Ze ぜ　So そ Zo ぞ

③ T with this added mark (゛) becomes d

た ta	becomes	→ だ da
ち chi		→ ぢ ji
つ tsu		→ づ zu
て te		→ で de
と to		→ ど do

Ta た Da だ　Chi ち Ji ぢ
Tsu つ Zu づ　Te て De で　To と Do ど

④ H with this added mark (゛) becomes b

は ha	becomes	→ ば ba
ひ hi		→ び bi
ふ fu		→ ぶ bu
へ he		→ べ be
ほ ho		→ ぼ bo

Ha は Ba ば　Hi ひ Bi び
Fu ふ Bu ぶ　He へ Be べ　Ho ほ Bo ぼ

⑤ H with this added mark (゜) becomes p

は ha	becomes	→ ぱ pa
ひ hi		→ ぴ pi
ふ fu		→ ぷ pu
へ he		→ ぺ pe
ほ ho		→ ぽ po

Ha は Ba ば Pa ぱ　Hi ひ Bi び Pi ぴ
Fu ふ Bu ぶ Pu ぷ　He へ Be べ Pe ぺ　Ho ほ Bo ぼ Po ぽ

24 Kana Combination Sound Changes

In order to form double sounds it takes a combination of two **kana** letters. Thus (**ki**-き) combined with a small (**ya**-ゃ) becomes (**kya**-きゃ), (**yu**-ゅ) becomes (**kyu**-きゅ) and so on. Notice the **kana** chart for more combinations.

きゃ kya	きゅ kyu	きょ kyo	ひゃ hya	ひゅ hyu	ひょ hyo	じゃ ja	じゅ ju	じょ jo
しゃ sha	しゅ shu	しょ sho	みゃ mya	みゅ myu	みょ myo	ぢゃ ja	ぢゅ ju	ぢょ jo
ちゃ cha	ちゅ chu	ちょ cho	りゃ rya	りゅ ryu	りょ ryo	びゃ bya	びゅ byu	びょ byo
にゃ nya	にゅ nyu	にょ nyo	ぎゃ gya	ぎゅ gyu	ぎょ gyo	ぴゃ pya	ぴゅ pyu	ぴょ pyo

Handakuon Transformation

Transformation of syllables begin with a tiny circular mark (゜) called **handakuon** or, (**han-nigori**) which is added to the upper right side of each semi-voiced syllable. Thus you transform (**p**) the counterpart of (**h**) and others in the following ways: (**ha**-は) becomes (pa-ぱ), (**fu**-ふ) becomes (**pu**-ぷ) and so on. Another use for these kana is that they are often printed in smaller type and placed next to specific kanji to show how the latter can be read and pronounced. Including the final consonant '**n**' the following compound sounds are all part of Japanese basic sounds: (**kya**), (**kyu**), (**kyo**), (**gya**), (**gyu**), (**gyo**), (**sha**), (**shu**) and (**sho**).

Vowel / Consonant	a	i	u	e	o
p	ぱ pa	ぴ pi	ぷ pu	ぺ pe	ぽ po

When writing them in **hiragana**, the syllable (**shi**-し) gets written as (**ji**-じ) and (**chi**-ち) is written as (**ji**-ぢ), making a pair, while (**su**-す) gets written as (**zu**-ず) and (**tsu**-つ) is written as (**zu**-づ) thus creating a second pair. In a few cases (じ) gets written as (ぢ) and (ず) gets written as (づ). The syllable (じ) (**katakana** ジ), not (ぢ) (**katakana** ヂ) is generally used to produce the sound (じ) except where the (**chi** ち) is changed into (じ) in a compound word or the sound '**ji**' is preceded by the sound '**chi**' in a word. In such a case (ぢ) (**katakana** ヂ) is used.

There is no difference in sound between the pairs (じ) and (ぢ)

and (ず) and (づ). What makes a slight difference is that (**ji** じ) and (**zu** ず) are ranked as more commonly used.

Examples :

Hiragana :	はなぢ	じしん	すずしい
Romaji :	**hanaji**	**jishin**	**suzushii**
English :	nose bleed	earthquake	cool

Exceptions :

Hiragana :	ちかづく	つづく	こどもづれ
Romaji :	**chikazuku**	**tsuzuku**	**kodomozure**
English :	close to	to continue	people with children

や **ya** ゆ **yu** よ **yo**

Their contorted or combination sounds (**Yō On**) are made by using a consonant plus the consonant '**y**' plus a vowel. Merely add '**y**' to make (**ya**-や), (**yu**-ゆ) or (**yo**-よ). Notice the chart to see how other syllables are made into combined sounds.

Formation Of Double Consonants

Hiragana	Katakana	Rōmaji
っ	ッ	kk, pp, ss, tch, tt

In reality, double consonants are actually a type of combined syllables. However, the importance of the distinction between a single and double consonant can't be stressed enough. Many words containing single consonants are apt to unintentionally receive a changed meaning, whenever they are mispronounced as double consonants. Thus the main rule to remember is that whenever the first sound of the second consonant is either (**k**), (**s**), (**sh**), (**ts**), (**ch**), (**f**) or (**h**) subsequently consonants double.

For instance except for (**mm**-) or (**nn**-), when a syllable ends in a consonant, by placing a small (**tsu**-っ) which is a complete syllable by itself, before a **kana** symbol beginning with either (**k**), (**s**), (**t**) or (**p**) you'll automatically create a double consonant. Furthermore, whenever a particular consonant occurs in sequence it results in the formation of a double consonant such as (**kk**), (**ss**), (**pp**), (**tt**), (**ssh**) or (**tch**). Notice how these double consonants are written.

26 Combined Consonant(s) Plus Vowel Sounds

The **'ts'** (considered a single compound consonant) and **'su'** syllables require the same length of pronunciation because they normally appear in sequence ; as in hats and eight rats.

ch, tsh and **sh** all produce a sound similar to church or fish.

Examples :

Single Consonants (made into →) Double Consonants

	Single Consonants	Double Consonants
Hiragana :	ようか	よっか
Romaji :	**yōka**	**yokka**
English :	The eighth	4 days/4th day

Hiragana :	じかん	じっかん
Romaji :	**jikan**	**jikkan**
English :	time	feeling

Hiragana :	かった	よんだって	いっしょ
Romaji :	**katta**	**yondatte**	**issho**
English :	bought it	He said to read	together

You must remember that when placed before **(h-)** you'll get a double **(pp-)** sound.

Examples :

Hiragana :	はっぽん	しゅっぱつ	いっぱい	でっぱ
Romaji :	**happon**	**shuppatsu**	**ippai**	**deppa**
English :	eight round objects	to start	one cup	buck teeth

(ki-き) or **(ku-く)** placed before a **(k)** brings about these examples.

Hiragana :	がっこう	はっきり	ひゃっかてん	ストッキング
Romaji :	**gakkō**	**hakkiri**	**hyakkaten**	**sutokkingu**
English :	school	clearly	department store	stocking

Pronunciation Notes

While pronouncing the double consonant in the word **'hakkiri'**, make a split second pause at **'ha'** with held breath for a full syllable before pronouncing **'kkiri'**.

An extremely difficult sound to imitate especially when it is at the beginning of a word, the **(tsu-つ)** pronunciation sound comes closest to the English word 'cats'.

When using **(chi-チ)** syllable, **(tsu-ッ)** is expressed by the Roman letter **(t)**.

Examples :

Katakana :	マッチ	キャッチャー	いっち
Romaji :	**matchi**	**Kyatchā**	**itchi**
English :	a match	catcher	accord

Hiragana : げ|つ two syllables
Romaji : **getsu**
English : month

Hiragana : ず|っ|と three syllables
Romaji : **zutto**
English : quite some time

Hiragana : ゆ|っ|く|り four syllables
Romaji : **yukkuri**
English : slowly

Making Use of The Syllabic Consonant ん(**n**)

The consonant sound '**n**'(**hiragana**-ん) (**katakana**-ン) which is not combined with any other vowel sound stands out as the only consonant that is a self-sustaining syllable representing itself as you'll notice in the kana chart. In Japanese grammar it is placed only before another consonant or at the end of a syllable in a word.

'n' gets pronounced differently depending on the sound that follows it. It gets pronounced as the **'ng'** in either 'gong' or 'sing' before (**t**), (**d**), (**r**), (**z**), (**chi**), (**j**) and (**n**) when not attached to a vowel.

Notice these particular points.

1) When at the end of a word it is pronounced nasally but at all other times like the **'n'** in 'English' or 'invention'.

Examples :

Hiragana :	でんぷん	ちかん	なんにん
Romaji :	**denpun**	**chikan**	**nan nin**
English :	starch	molester	how many people ?

2) In the middle of a word when followed by a consonant it gets pronounced as an independent consonant sound.

28 Combined Consonant (s) Plus Vowel Sounds

Examples :

Hiragana :	きんえん
Romaji :	**kin-en**
English :	no smoking

A final **'n'** placed before a syllable with an initial **'n'** always doubles the consonant and takes a syllabic nasal sound in any word paired with a **'n'**.

Examples :

Hiragana :	そんな	あんな
Romaji :	**sonna**	**anna**
English :	that way	that

3) When **'n'** is followed by syllables beginning with **(b)**, **(m)** or **(p)** it is pronounced more like **'m'** and is also written as **(mm-)** or **(nn-)**.

Examples :

Hiragana :	さんぽ	せんもん	さんばんせん
Romaji :	**sampo**	**semmon**	**samban-sen**
English :	a stroll	specialty	track 3
Hiragana :	しんぶん	こんにちは	ぎんこう
Romaji :	**shimbun**	**konnichi wa**	**ginkō**
English :	newspaper	hello	bank

Introduction To The Two Ways Of Romanizing Japanese

Romaji is the term used to indicate a system of applying the Roman alphabet to spell native Japanese words as well as Japanese loan words. Since it is practically impossible to transliterate with real accuracy all Japanese pronunciation in Roman letters, learners will have to make do with one of the two Romanization systems currently in existence.

Dr. Aikitsu Tanakadate and Dr. Takuro Tamaru first started their version of a Romanization system in 1905. This was superceded by the so-called Kunrei-shiki (Official System, or Government System) which made its appearance in 1946, but proved unsuccessful and ineffective. Although it is used in Japanese primary schools and in some Romanized basic Japanese language learning books, some awfully strange pronunciation can emanate from the mouths of users, not to mention some strange spellings. For example, something to cause a titter would be this : The name of an area in Tokyo is called Chichibu under the Hepburn system and in the Government System it is rendered as 'titti-boo.'

The Hepburn Romanization System used in this book to make it easier for English speakers to learn Japanese more quickly is named after its inventor Dr. James Curtis Hepburn (1815-1911). An American Presbyterian medical missionary, he came to Japan in 1859. The third edition of his enlarged and completely revised Japanese-English and English-Japanese Dictionary was published in 1886 in Yokohama. He returned to America in 1892, but what he left behind has proven so consistently effective that it is a widely used method for transcribing written Japanese into Roman style letters.

This system is universally employed to Romanize all the names of Japan's railways and subway stations, as well as most Japanese firms, banks and hotels. It is used in the Romanization of Japanese-English dictionaries, as an aid in basic lessons for persons who are first studying Japanese until they are able to master hiragana, and also widely used in newspapers, books, advertisements and magazines within and outside Japan.

Do be aware of the fact that as the result of the existence of these competing systems, very few Japanese are consistent in Romanizing Japanese. Thus capitalization and division of Romanized words also vary rampantly. Other additional uses of Romanized letters are for producing signs, for making abbreviations and pointing out units of measure.

30 Basic Kana (あ-Ah) To (お-O) Stroke Order

arukimashō!
let's walk!

arukitai
want to walk

aruke nai
can't walk

isoida
hurried

isoide
in a hurry

isoide iru
am hurrying

saishūeki
last station

kono eki
this station

tsugi no eki
next station

eshaku suru
I bow my head

utau
sing

utatta
sang

utau deshō
will sing

okashii
is funny

okashiku furumau
acts funny

okashiku mieru
looks funny

THREE **STROKES**

Today's Target Kana For Stroke Practice

あ	ア
Hiragana Soft Cursive Writing	Katakana Stiff Square Strokes

Next Kana

い

I

Hints For Stroke Order Reproduction And Recognition

(あ-**ah**) is the pronunciation for this kana. It is roughly pronounced like the '**ah**' in father but don't open your mouth as wide. Avoid Kana Similarity Problems. Although the top stroke is the same for the kana (あ-**a**) and (ま-**ma**), notice the next two strokes for both kana. Beware of the loops. Be sure to write each kana accurately less one be mistaken for the other.

Target Strokes	1	2	3	4	5	6	7	8	9
あ			あ						
ア		ア							

TWO STROKES

Today's Target Kana For Stroke Practice

Last Kana	Hiragana Soft Cursive Writing	Katakana Stiff Square Strokes	Next Kana
あ	い	イ	う
A			U

Hints For Stroke Order Reproduction And Recognition

(い-e) is the pronunciation sound for this kana. It is pronounced like the vowel in 'eat' but is shorter and slightly strained. Avoid Kana Similarity Problems. (い-i) is sometimes mistaken for (り-ri) by many beginners and even advanced students of Japanese as a second language. The right stroke of (い-i) is shorter than its left stroke but it is just the opposite for (り-ri).

Target Strokes	1	2	3	4	5	6	7	8	9
い		い							
イ	ノ	イ							

TWO STROKES

Today's Target Kana For Stroke Practice

Last Kana	Hiragana	Katakana	Next Kana
い	う	ウ	え
I	Soft Cursive Writing	Stiff Square Strokes	E

Hints For Stroke Order Reproduction And Recognition

(う-**u**) is the pronunciation sound for this kana. It's similar to the vowel in 'cool' except you should spread rather than round your lips. Avoid Kana Similarity Problems. These two kana look alike and are the same in pronunciation but remember, one is **hiragana** while the other is **katakana**.

Target Strokes	1	2	3	4	5	6	7	8	9
う		う							
ウ			ウ						

TWO STROKES

Today's Target Kana For Stroke Practice

Last Kana	Hiragana	Katakana	Next Kana
う	え	エ	お
U	Hiragana Soft Cursive Writing	Katakana Stiff Square Strokes	O

Hints For Stroke Order Reproduction And Recognition

(え-**eh**) is the pronunciation sound for this kana. 'E' is pronounced like the vowel in 'egg' but don't open your mouth too wide. For the best stroke writing results, use a felt tip pen. Then start from the left and follow the arrows. Using the very first kana as an example, slowly, with a light steady hand try to accurately form your target kana. Use all the blank box spaces and imitate the strokes of your present and last kana until your kana resemble the original ones.

Target Strokes	1	2	3	4	5	6	7	8	9
え	`	え							
エ	一	T	エ						

THREE STROKES

Today's Target Kana For Stroke Practice

Last Kana	Hiragana Soft Cursive Writing	Katakana Stiff Square Strokes	Next Kana
え	お	オ	か
E			KA

Hints For Stroke Order Reproduction And Recognition

(お-o) is the pronunciation sound for this kana. Its sound is similar to that in the vowel for 'go' except that the lips are rounded less. For the best stroke writing results, use a felt tip pen. Then start from the left and follow the arrows. Using the very first kana as an example, slowly, with a light steady hand try to accurately form your target kana. Use all the blank box spaces and imitate the strokes of your present and last kana until your kana resemble the original ones. After five strokes you'll be able to write your first word. Now that you have learned the first five kana, you are able to write your first words. Congratulations !

Target Strokes	1	2	3	4	5	6	7	8	9
お	⼀	お	お						
オ	一	才	オ						

Basic Kana (あ-Ah) To (お-O) Stroke Order

CREATIVE KANA REVIEW

Write it! Read it! Say it!

あ	い	う	え	お
A	I	U	E	O

LINK-A-LETTER: You have already practiced writing all the hiragana on this page. Now use them to build new words in the adjoining boxes. Then try to link them to phrases.

あい **ai** love	いう **iu** say
あお **ao** blue	いえ **ie** house
あう **au** meet	うえ **ue** up
いい **ii** good	え **e** picture
い **i** stomach	おい **oi** nephew

Stroke Guidance Review 37

(Point Out What's Wrong)

Remembering what you have already read regarding stroke order, carefully notice how some strokes are written. See how you measure up.

This → め is the correct stroke for → 

Carefully notice how the correct stroke begins and ends. Now check and see what you may have done wrong or right. Check one box with an 'X'.

This stroke あ is wrong because it was written

Above the line ☐ Below the line ☐ It's okay ☐

This stroke に is wrong because it was drawn

Too short ☐ Too long ☐ It's okay ☐

The correct stroke line  goes upwards

To the right ☐ To the left ☐ It's okay ☐

Put a check mark below each wrongly stroked kana and write the correct way it should appear in the spare boxes and pronounce each kana aloud with your Japanese 'kana helpmate'.

Review strokes →	を	は	け	や
Your written stroke →				

38 Vocabulary Expanding For Interacting

Talking About Names

NATURAL SURVIVAL CONVERSATION

What You Might Hear	How You Might Possibly Answer
(P) **Ano kata no o namae wa nan desu ka ?** (E) What is her name ?	(P) **Ano kata no namae wa Amado Fuaiza desu. Amado ga sei desu.** (E) Her name is Ahmad, Faiza. Ahmad is her family name.
(P) **Dochira ga sei dato wakarimasu ka ?** (E) How can we know which is the family name ?	(P) **Nihongo o hanashitari kaitari suru toki wa, sei o saki ni shimasu.** (E) When speaking or writing Japanese, the family name is used first.
(P) **Kaitari ittari suru toki dochira ga sei desu ka ?** (M) When writing or saying your name, which is the family name ?	(P) **Watashi no namae wa Zana Faya desu. Sei wa Faya desu.** (E) My name is Zana Faya. My family name is Faya.
(P) **O namae wa dō yū fū ni kakimasu ka ?** (E) How do you spell your name ?	(P) **S-h-a-z-a-a-r to kakimasu.** (E) It's spelt S-h-a-z-a-a-r.
(P) **Kare no ojōsan wa kurasu de ichiban yoku dekiru ko desu ka ?** (E) Isn't his daughter the smartest in her class ?	(P) **Iie, watashi no musume no Akiko ga ichiban desu.** (E) No, she isn't. My daughter Akiko is.
(O) **Kiichi wa seki o shita toki ni seki kara ochita.** (M) When Kiichi coughed he fell off the chair.	(O) **Eki-sha ga itta tōri da.** (M) The fortune-teller said that would happen.
(O) **Fumio-san no suekko wa sengetsu no sue ni umaremashita.** (E) Mr. Fumio's youngest child was born at the end of last month.	(O) **Nigatsu wa mijikai tsuki desu.** (E) February is a short month.
(O) **Hiroko, naze kesa watashi o mushi shita no ?** (E) Hiroko, why did you ignore me this morning ?	(C) **Datte himitsu o mamorenai kara.** (E) Because you can't keep a secret.

Vocabulary Expanding For Interacting

Talking About Names

NATURAL SURVIVAL CONVERSATION

What You Might Hear	How You Might Possibly Answer
(C) **Kita-san ga kita toki futon ga futtonda.** (E) When Mr. North came, the bedding had blown away.	(O) **Honto ni Minami-san wa doka nakatta no ?** (W) Are you sure Miss South didn't remove it ?
(O) **Hiroshi wa ato de Itsuko to issho ni suiei ni ikitagatte iru.** (E) Hiroshi wants to go swimming later with Itsuko.	(O) **Itsuko wa ikitaku nai node tsukareta furi o shite iru.** (E) Itsuko doesn't want to go, so she's pretending she's tired.
(O) **Hiromi, denwa wa dare ga deta ?** (E) Hiromi, who answered the phone ?	(O) **Denwakyoku no hito ga denwa ni deta.** (M) The telephone man answered the phone.
(C) **Eriko, jan-jan nomōze.** (M) Eriko, let's go and get drunk.	(O) **Dame, anata wa ōusotsuki da kara.** (W) No, because you're a professional liar.

Twist Your Tongue With These Tongue Twisters

3) Bōsan ga byōbu ni jōzu na bōzu no bōshi no e o kaita.
A buddhist priest drew a good picture of a priest's hat on the upright screen.

4) Chagama amagappa akagama amagappa.
Brown pan, raincoat, red pan and raincoat.

40 Basic Kana (か-Ka) To (こ-Ko) Stroke Order

kane o ageta
gave money

kane o morau
received money

Itareri tsukuseri no osewa ni kokoro kara kansha shitemasu.
I'm truly grateful for all your heart-warming help.

Ki o tsukete.
Take care of yourself.

Kikanakatta.
I didn't hear it.

Kinō wa yoku furimashita ne.
It rained a lot yesterday, didn't it?

kutsu o haku
put on shoes

kutsu o nugu
take off shoes

kumo ga kirai
dislike spiders

kemuri ga kirai
dislike smoke

kenka suru na
don't fight

korobashita
made it fall

korobu deshō
will fall

THREE STROKES

Today's Target Kana For Stroke Practice

Last Kana	Hiragana	Katakana	Next Kana
お	か	カ	き
O	Hiragana Soft Cursive Writing	Katakana Stiff Square Strokes	KI

Hints For Stroke Order Reproduction And Recognition

(か-**ka**) is the pronunciation sound for this kana. For the best stroke writing results, use a felt tip pen. Then start from the left and follow the arrows. Using the very first kana as an example, slowly, with a light steady hand try to accurately form your target kana. Use all the blank box spaces and imitate the strokes of your present and last kana until your kana resemble the original ones.

Target Strokes	1	2	3	4	5	6	7	8	9

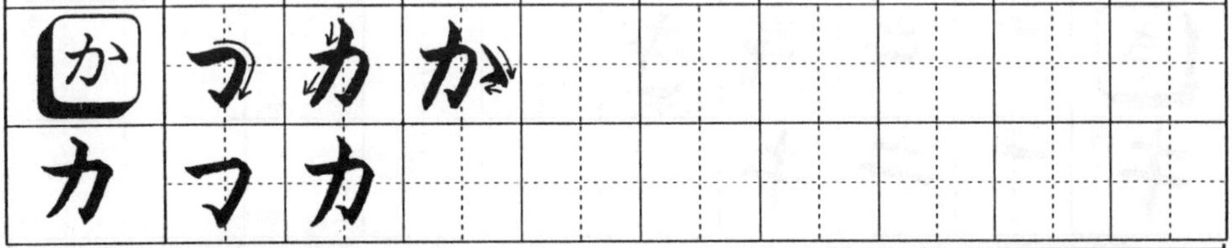

FOUR STROKES

Today's Target Kana For Stroke Practice

Last Kana	Hiragana	Katakana	Next Kana
か	き	キ	く
KA	Hiragana Soft Cursive Writing	Katakana Stiff Square Strokes	KU

Hints For Stroke Order Reproduction And Recognition

(き-**ki**) is the pronunciation sound for this kana. For the best stroke writing results, use a felt tip pen. Then start from the left and follow the arrows. Using the very first kana as an example, slowly, with a light steady hand try to accurately form your target kana. Use all the blank box spaces and imitate the strokes of your present and last kana until your kana resemble the original ones.

Target Strokes	1	2	3	4	5	6	7	8	9
き									
キ									

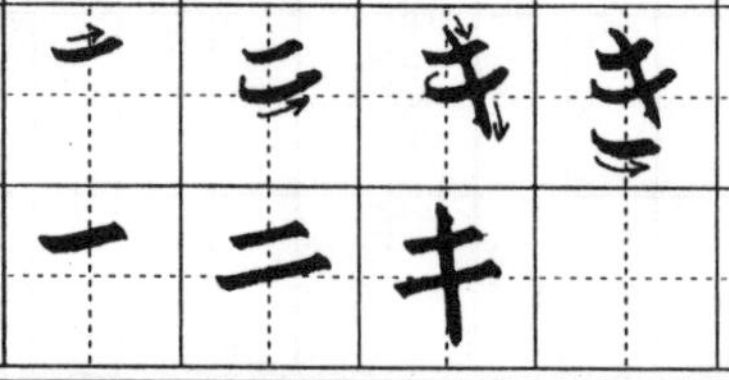

ONE STROKE

Today's Target Kana For Stroke Practice

Last Kana	Hiragana Soft Cursive Writing	Katakana Stiff Square Strokes	Next Kana
き	く	ク	け
KI			KE

Hints For Stroke Order Reproduction And Recognition

(く-**ku**) is the pronunciation sound for this kana. Avoid Kana Similarity Problems. (**ku**) is a vertical standup one-stroke kana whereby (へ-**he**) is drawn into the form of a long angular wide right horizontal shaped kana.

Target Strokes	1	2	3	4	5	6	7	8	9
く	く								
ク	ノ	ク							

THREE STROKES

Today's Target Kana For Stroke Practice

Last Kana			Next Kana
く	け	ケ	こ
KU	Hiragana Soft Cursive Writing	Katakana Stiff Square Strokes	KO

Hints For Stroke Order Reproduction And Recognition

(け-**ke**) is the pronunciation sound for this kana. Avoid Kana Similarity Problems. These two kana almost look alike and are the same in pronunciation, but remember, one is hiragana while the other is katakana.

Target Strokes	1	2	3	4	5	6	7	8	9
け	I	に	け						
ケ	ノ	ト	ケ						

TWO		Today's Target Kana For Stroke Practice		STROKES
Last Kana				Next Kana
け	こ		コ	さ
	Hiragana Soft Cursive Writing		Katakana Stiff Square Strokes	
KE				SA

Hints For Stroke Order Reproduction And Recognition

(こ-**ko**) is the pronunciation sound of this kana. Avoid Kana Similarity Problems. Though these two kana look alike, being hiragana and katakana is what sets them apart. The strokes for (こ-**ko**) are slightly horizontal but the strokes for (い-**i**) are more vertical. For the katakana (コ-**ko**) the bottom horizontal stroke comes to an even halt at the base of the vertical stroke, for the katakana (ユ-**yu**) the final horizontal stroke is drawn a little further.

Target Strokes	1	2	3	4	5	6	7	8	9
こ									
コ									

Basic Kana (か-Ka) To (こ-Ko) Stroke Order

CREATIVE KANA REVIEW

Write it! Read it! Say it!

か	き	く	け	こ
KA	KI	KU	KE	KO

LINK-A-LETTER: You have already practiced writing all the hiragana on this page. Now use them to build new words in the adjoining boxes. Then try to link them to phrases.

かく **kaku** write					かお **kao** face				
きく **kiku** hear					こい **koi** love				
くう **kuu** eat					ここ **koko** here				
かい **kai** shell					か **ka** mosquito				
こえ **koe** voice					かき **kaki** persimmon				

SEARCH AND MATCH IDENTICAL KANA 47

Expand your kana recognition ability. Search within the numbers (1-5) for the kana which matches the left hand column Romanized letters. Write the correct kana in the blank boxes. Then use the bottom page boxes to practice any kana you wish.

EXAMPLE:

			1	2	3	4	5
		Answer	↓	↓	↓	↓	↓
ga	←	3	だ	な	が	み	ぱ

Mark your correct answer numbers in these boxes below			1	2	3	4	5
		⬇	⬇	⬇	⬇	⬇	⬇
i	⬅		ひ	い	り	し	け
ku	⬅		う	し	い	く	へ
me	⬅		れ	ね	め	わ	ぬ
ra	⬅		ら	ち	う	と	る
fu	⬅		ぶ	え	ぬ	め	ふ

Practice writing any kana in these boxes

48 Vocabulary Expanding For Interacting

Casual Kitchen Table Talk

NATURAL SURVIVAL CONVERSATION

What You Might Hear	How You Might Possibly Answer
(O) **Konya wa ima made ni itta koto ga nai tokoro e ikitai.** (W) Tonight I'd like to go somewhere I've never been before.	(C) **Shukō o kaete daidokoro ni iku yō ni shitara.** (E) Why not try the kitchen for a change!
(P) **Watashi wa katei ryōri no nioi ga suki desu.** (E) I like the smell of home cooked food.	(O) **Chōmiryō ga zenzen arimasen.** (E) I'm all out of condiments for cooking.
(P) **Nan-deshitara watashi ga katte mairimashō ka?** (E) Then shall I go and buy some?	(O) **Itsumo sugu tetsudatte kuremasu ne!** (E) You're always quick to lend a helping hand.
(O) **Mizu ga pota-pota to jaguchi kara dete imasu.** (E) Drops of water are trickling from the faucet.	(O) **Isoide naoshite agemasu.** (E) I'll fix it quickly.
(P) **Tomodachi kara omiyage ni moratta manaita wa doko ni arimasu-ka?** (E) Where's the chopping board I received as a gift from my friend?	(P) **Watashi ga shimaimashita.** (E) I put it away.
(C) **Boku wa paku-paku nan demo itadakimasu.** (M) I'm so hungry I could eat anything.	(P) **Kono hotto keiki o hera de hikkuri kaesu made matte kudasai.** (E) Please wait until I turn over the pancake with this spatula.
(O) **Hotto keiki ni tsukeru toketa batā o kuremasu ka?** (E) Can you give me some melted butter to put on top of the pancakes?	(P) **Hai, tsumetai nomimono wa ikaga desu ka?** (E) Yes. How about something cold to drink?
(O) **Kono naifu wa kirenaku natta.** (E) This knife has become dull.	(O) **Togiya no tokoro e motte iku to kireru yō ni naru.** (M) I'll take it to the knife sharpener.

NATURAL SURVIVAL CONVERSATION

What You Might Hear	How You Might Possibly Answer
(C) **Omiotsuke mō ippai kureru?** (E) Can you give me another helping of soybean soup?	(VP) **Dōzo meshiagatte kudasai.** (E) Yes, please have some more.
(O) **Chotto ryōri no puro mo kaomake desu.** (E) To a certain degree you put a professional cook to shame.	(O) **Chōdo sore o iō to shite ita.** (M) You took the words right out of my mouth.
(O) **Tezukuri no bureddo-pudingu o taberaretara ii na to omou.** (E) I sure wish I could taste some homemade bread pudding.	(C) **Nan-nara watashi ga....** (E) Shall I make some?
(P) **Ryōri suru no o yasumasete itada-ku.** (E) I'm giving myself a rest from cook-ing.	(P) **Oryōri to sara arai o tetsudatte agemasu.** (W) Then I'll cook and wash the dishes.
(O) **Kare wa suisen benjo ni suisen o ikeru yō ni suisen shita.** (M) He recommended that I put the daffodils in the flush toilet.	(P) **Watashi wa mainichi shokubutsu ni mizu o yarimasu.** (E) I water the house plants everyday.
(C) **Kocchi o muite kono okurimono o akete kurenai.** (E) Won't you turn around and open this present.	(C) **Waku-waku suru.** (E) My heart is pounding with anticipa-tion.

50 Basic Kana (さ-Sa) To (そ-So) Stroke Order

Sara ga ochita.
The plates fell down.

Sake o nonde iru.
I'm drinking rice wine.

Sawaru na!
Don't touch!

Suika o tabete iru.
I'm eating watermelon.

Sumi ni okenai yatsu da.
You have to be careful of him.

Subete wa itareri tsukuseri deshita.
Everything was perfect!

Shita o muku.
Look down.

Shigatsu wa atatakai.
April is warm.

Kono shigoto wa tema ga kakaru.
This work requires a lot of time.

Soko ni oite kudasai.
Please place it there.

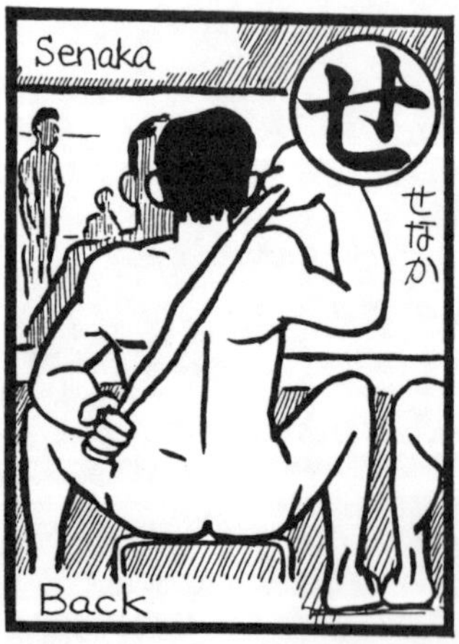

Soen ni natta.
We're no longer in touch.

Senaka ga kayui.
My back itches.

seiyōjin
Westerners

Sentaku o suru.
I'm doing laundry.

THREE STROKES

Today's Target Kana For Stroke Practice

Last Kana			Next Kana
こ	さ	サ	し
KO	Hiragana Soft Cursive Writing	Katakana Stiff Square Strokes	SHI

Hints For Stroke Order Reproduction And Recognition

(さ-**sa**), which is the pronunciation of this kana, has a little less aspiration than its nearest corresponding English equivalent. Avoid Kana Similarity Problems. Whereas (さ-**sa**) requires one horizontal stroke, (き-**ki**) requires two strokes.

Target Strokes	1	2	3	4	5	6	7	8	9
さ			さ						
サ	一	十	サ						

ONE	Today's Target Kana For Stroke Practice		STROKE
Last Kana			Next Kana
さ	し	シ	す
	Hiragana Soft Cursive Writing	Katakana Stiff Square Strokes	
SA			SU

Hints For Stroke Order Reproduction And Recognition

(し-**shi**), the pronunciation sound of this kana, though sounding like the English "she", requires less rounding of the lips. Avoid Kana Similarity Problems. (し-**shi**) which looks like a hook, is formed by initially drawing a vertical stroke and then curving it at its base. The horizontally drawn (つ-**tsu**) stroke has a curved base pointing in the opposite direction of (し-**shi**). When forming the katakana (シ-**shi**) stroke, the first stroke is started from the bottom and thins out at the top, while the final stroke for (ツ-**tsu**) is drawn by starting from the top and thins out at its base. Whereas (ツ-**tsu**) has three strokes (ソ-**so**) has only two strokes.

Target Strokes	1	2	3	4	5	6	7	8	9
し	し								
シ	丶	冫	シ						

TWO STROKES

Today's Target Kana For Stroke Practice

Last Kana	Hiragana Soft Cursive Writing	Katakana Stiff Square Strokes	Next Kana
し	す	ス	せ
SHI			SE

Hints For Stroke Order Reproduction And Recognition

(す-**su**), the pronunciation for this kana, is similar to the English "Sue" in sound. Avoid Kana Similarity Problems: As you will notice, the last stroke of the katakana(ス-**su**) is drawn midway on the right. However, the katakana(ヌ-**nu**) has a slanted stroke right at its mid-section.

Target Strokes	1	2	3	4	5	6	7	8	9
す	一	す							
ス	フ	ス							

THREE STROKES

Today's Target Kana For Stroke Practice

Last Kana			Next Kana
す	せ	セ	そ
SU	Hiragana Soft Cursive Writing	Katakana Stiff Square Strokes	SO

Hints For Stroke Order Reproduction And Recognition

(せ-**se**), the pronunciation for this kana, is similar to the 'ce' in the English "celery". Avoid Kana Similarity Problems : These two kana look alike, but the fact that one is hiragana and the other is katakana distinguishes one from the other, even though they are pronounced the same.

Target Strokes	1	2	3	4	5	6	7	8	9
せ	一	十	せ						
セ	フ	セ							

TWO STROKES

Today's Target Kana For Stroke Practice

Last Kana	Hiragana	Katakana	Next Kana
せ	そ	ソ	た
SE	Hiragana Soft Cursive Writing	Katakana Stiff Square Strokes	TA

Hints For Stroke Order Reproduction And Recognition

(そ-**so**), the pronunciation of this kana, is similar to the English "sew". For the best stroke writing results, use a felt tip pen. Start from the left and follow the arrows. Using the very first kana as an example, slowly, with a light steady hand, try to accurately form your target kana. Use all blank box spaces and imitate the strokes of your present and last kana until your kana resemble the original ones.

Target Strokes	1	2	3	4	5	6	7	8	9
そ									
ソ									

CREATIVE KANA REVIEW

Write it! Read it! Say it!

さ	し	す	せ	そ
SA	SHI	SU	SE	SO

LINK-A-LETTER: You have already practiced writing all the hiragana on this page. Now use them to build new words in the adjoining boxes. Then try to link them to phrases.

さけ **sake** rice wine					せかい **sekai** world				
そうか **sō ka** understand					さか **saka** slope				
すこし **sukoshi** a little					そこ **soko** that place				
しか **shika** deer					し **shi** city				
すき **suki** fond of					しお **shio** salt				

HERE'S A NEW, SIMPLE, FUN WAY TO LEARN LETTERS AND WORDS CREATIVELY, WHILE SAMPLING SOME OF JAPAN'S CULTURE. HIRAGANA IDEOGRAMS ARE MISSING IN THE BOXES ABOVE THE ROMANIZED VERSION OF THEIR SOUNDS. TO COMPLETE A WORD, MERELY DIP INTO THE LETTER BOX CONTAINING ALL THE LETTERS NEEDED. AFTER THAT, WITH THE POSSIBLE HELP OF EITHER A JAPANESE ACQUAINTANT OR A ROMANIZED DICTIONARY, GROUP ALL THE WORDS INTO A SENTENCE.

Example :
Hot barley tea **(mugicha)** tastes good in the wintertime. (ぎ) is the missing letter for box number two. Write it.

1	2	3
む		ちゃ
MU	**GI**	**CHA**

Now you can dig into the letter box for letters to fill in the boxes below.

Quizzeria

1) A popular seafood snack of Japan.

	し
SU	**SHI**

2) Japanese wipe their faces with it.

お	し		
O	**SHI**	**BO**	**RI**

3) It is entered into for bathing.

お		ろ
O	**FU**	**RO**

58 Vocabulary Expanding For Interacting

Same Sounding Words

NATURAL SURVIVAL CONVERSATION

What You Might Hear	How You Might Possibly Answer
(O) **Sakuban gokiburi o takusan korو-shimashita.** (E) Last night I killed a lot of cockroaches.	(P) **Ni-san biki oikakeru aida ni korobimashita.** (E) I stumbled while chasing a few.
(O) **Kare wa hen na ningen desu.** (E) He's a strange person.	(O) **Takusan ninjin taberu kara kai?** (M) Is that because he eats lots of carrots?
(O) **Watashitachi wa kanojo ga goshujin to issho ni iru no o mita koto ga nai.** (E) We never see her with her husband.	(O) **Kare ga shūjin dakara.** (E) That's because he's in prison.
(O) **Kanji o kaku renshū o shite imasu.** (E) I am learning to write Chinese characters.	(O) **Sonna benkyō o suru kanji niwa ichido mo narimasen.** (E) I'm never in the mood to study.
(O) **Kana o futatsuki de oboerare masu ka?** (E) Is it possible to learn kana in two months?	(O) **Sō ka na?** (E) Is that so? *(or)* That may be possible.
(O) **Ima ware-ware wa eikaiwa o benkyō shite imasu.** (E) We are studying English now.	(C) **Watashi wa kanji o kakenakute ya na kanji.** (E) I feel bad because I can't write Japanese characters.
(P) **Natsu ni nani ga hoshii desu ka?** (E) What do you want for summer?	(O) **Sora no hoshi o miru kikai ga hoshii.** (E) I want a chance to look at the stars in the sky!
(C) **Sono ryōri wa umakatta.** (M) That food was delicious.	(C) **Ryōri-chō ga umai kara.** (M) That's because the chef is good.

NATURAL SURVIVAL CONVERSATION

What You Might Hear	How You Might Possibly Answer
(P) **Tamanegi no kawa o muku no wa dōshitara ichiban ii desu ka?** (E) What's the best way to peel an onion?	(O) **Tamanegi o muku ichiban ii hōhō wa mizu no naka de muku koto desu.** (E) The best way to peel an onion is under water.
(O) **Watashi wa anata no hikkoshi no tame waza-waza jōkyō shita.** (E) I came just for the purpose of helping you to move.	(P) **Sore wa sore wa tōi tokoro o go-kurōsama deshita.** (E) Thank you for coming such a long way.
(O) **Karera wa hiso-hiso to hanashite iru.** (E) They're talking in hushed tones.	(P) **Tottemo jūyō na hito datta kara desu.** (E) That's because he's a very important man.
(C) **Irasshai-irasshai, dore demo hyaku-en desu.** (E) Welcome! Everything you see is 100 yen.	(O) **Zettai ni sō desu ka?** (E) Are you absolutely sure?
(O) **Matsuri no toki nihonjin wa wasshoi-wasshoi to sakebu.** (E) Japanese shout "Heave ho! Heave ho!" at festivals.	(C) **Kuwashiku hanashite kudasai.** (E) Really? Give me more in details.

Twist Your Tongue With These Tongue Twisters

5) **Den deraruru nara, dete kuru batten den derarenken denken konken konkorarenken korarera renkenkon.**
If I could have gone out I would have gone out. But since I can get out, I'm staying in. As I can't get out, I don't go out.

60 Basic Kana (た–Ta) To (と–To) Stroke Order

Tatami ni suwatte iru.
I'm sitting on straw mats.

Tamago o yuderu.
I'm boiling eggs.

Chiisai desu.
It's small.

Chikara ippai yatte iru.
I'm doing my best.

Tsumara nai hito da.
He's not an interesting person.

Zuibun tsuyoki desune.
You certainly have a lot of confidence.

To o tatakinasai.
Knock on the door.

Tochi ga takai.
Land is expensive.

Te o dasu na!
Don't bother it.

Tegirekin o harau.
I'm paying finalizing money.

FOUR STROKES

Today's Target Kana For Stroke Practice

Last Kana	Hiragana Soft Cursive Writing	Katakana Stiff Square Strokes	Next Kana
そ	た	タ	ち
SO			CHI

Hints For Stroke Order Reproduction And Recognition

(た-**ta**) is the pronunciation of this kana. While uttering this sound, the tip of the tongue touches the back of the front teeth and gum. This applies to all the other four kana of this '**t**' group. Not as much pressure is used for their sound as is used for the English equivalent consonant.

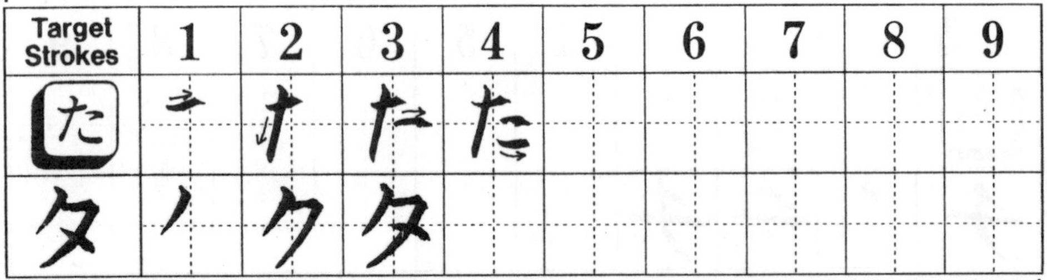

TWO STROKES

Today's Target Kana For Stroke Practice

Last Kana	Hiragana Soft Cursive Writing	Katakana Stiff Square Strokes	Next Kana
た	ち	チ	つ
TA			TSU

Hints For Stroke Order Reproduction And Recognition

(ち-**chi**), like in the 'chi' of "cheese", is the pronunciation of this kana. 'Chi' is often voiceless. For the best stroke writing results, use a felt tip pen. Then start from the left and follow the arrows. Using the very first kana as an example, slowly, with a light steady hand, try to accurately form your target kana. Use all the blank box spaces and imitate the strokes of your present and last kana until your kana resemble the original ones.

Target Strokes	1	2	3	4	5	6	7	8	9
ち									
チ									

ONE STROKE

Today's Target Kana For Stroke Practice

Last Kana			Next Kana
ち	つ	ツ	て
CHI	Hiragana Soft Cursive Writing	Katakana Stiff Square Strokes	TE

Hints For Stroke Order Reproduction And Recognition

(つ-**tsu**), like the 'ts' in "it's", is the pronunciation of this kana. For the best stroke writing results, use a felt tip pen. Then start from the left and follow the arrows. Using the very first kana as an example, slowly, with a light steady hand, try to accurately form your target kana. Use all the blank box spaces and imitate the strokes of your present and last kana until your kana resemble the original ones.

Target Strokes	1	2	3	4	5	6	7	8	9
つ	つ								
ツ	ヽ	ヽヽ	ツ						

ONE STROKE

Today's Target Kana For Stroke Practice

Last Kana			Next Kana
つ	て	テ	と
TSU	Hiragana Soft Cursive Writing	Katakana Stiff Square Strokes	TO

Hints For Stroke Order Reproduction And Recognition

(て-**te**), like the '**te**' in "tennis", is the pronunciation sound for this kana. Avoid Kana Similarity Problems. (**te**), if drawn slanted with a small curve like this (て) could be mistaken for (へ-**he**). Also, if its curve is too rounded and is made to look like this (フ) then it may be mistaken for (こ-**ko**) so be sure to write it in its proper form. The final stroke for the katakana (テ-**te**) starts vertically from the middle and curves midway to its base. But for the katakana (ラ-**ra**) the final stroke immediately starts to curve from its top right joint to its base.

Target Strokes	1	2	3	4	5	6	7	8	9
て	て								
テ	一	二	テ						

TWO STROKES

Today's Target Kana For Stroke Practice

Last Kana	Hiragana Soft Cursive Writing	Katakana Stiff Square Strokes	Next Kana
て	と	ト	な
TE			NA

Hints For Stroke Order Reproduction And Recognition

(と-**to**), like the English word "toe", is the pronunciation of this kana. For the best stroke writing results, use a felt tip pen. Start from the left and follow the arrows. Using the very first kana as an example, slowly, with a light steady hand, try to accurately form your target kana. Use all the blank box spaces and imitate the strokes of your present and last kana until your kana resemble the original ones.

Target Strokes	1	2	3	4	5	6	7	8	9
と		と							
ト		ト							

Basic Kana (た-Ta) To (と-To) Stroke Order

CREATIVE KANA REVIEW
Write it! Read it! Say it!

た	ち	つ	て	と
TA	CHI	TU	TE	TO

LINK-A-LETTER: You have already practiced writing all the hiragana on this page. Now use them to build new words in the adjoining boxes. Then try to link them to phrases.

て **te** a hand				とき **toki** time			
たしか **tashika** certainly				とし **toshi** age			
とうとう **tōtō** finally				とうい **tōi** far			
つい **tsui** just				たけ **take** bamboo			
たく **taku** boil rice				とけい **tokei** clock			

67 Some Basic Kanji To Recognize

68

Vocabulary Expanding For Interacting

Use of To Do (Suru) And Become (Naru)

NATURAL SURVIVAL CONVERSATION

What You Might Hear	How You Might Possibly Answer
(O) **Ima kara sōji o suru.** (E) I'm going to clean the house from now.	(P) **Dōzo go-jiyū ni.** (E) Please feel free to do so.
(O) **Ima kara shokuji o suru.** (E) I'm going to cook from now.	(O) **Watashi no ryōri wa mazui desu. Anata no ryōri wa oishii desu.** (E) My cooking is awful. I'm sure your's is delicious.
(O) **Mō sugu aki ni naru.** (E) Autumn will set in soon.	(C) **Motto natsu ga nagakereba yokatta no ni.** (E) It would be nice if summer lasted a little longer.
(O) **Kiotsuke-nakereba byōki ni naru.** (E) If you're not careful you'll become sick.	(C) **Nani o kiotsukereba iin desu ka ?** (E) What do I have to be careful of ?
(O) **Nani ka wasureta yō na ki ga suru.** (E) Somehow I feel I've forgotten something.	(C) **Jūdai dewa nakatta deshō.** (E) It can't have been very important.
(O) **Nagai aida ōatari o matta no de ima mune ga ippai ni naru.** (E) I've waited a long time for the big win and now I have a lump in my throat.	(O) **Kōun wa happō fusagari ni naru to omou hito ni otozureru.** (E) Good fortune sometimes comes to those who think there's no way out.
(C) **Hayatochiri suru.** (E) You think you understand but you don't.	(C) **Ichiban tsugō no warui toki ni kenbōshō ni kakatta yō desu ne !** (E) Lately you seem to have amnesia at the most inopportune time.
(P) **Dōshite nyūmon shite sugu yamemashita ka ?** (E) Why did you stop at the first lesson ?	(C) **Yaruki ga nai.** (E) I lost the will to continue.
(O) **Kanojo wa kare no kao o miru tabi ni odo odo suru.** (E) She acts frightened everytime she sees him.	(C) **Kare mo onaji da yo.** (M) So does he.

Vocabulary Expanding For Interacting

Use of To Do (Suru) And Become (Naru)

NATURAL SURVIVAL CONVERSATION

What You Might Hear	How You Might Possibly Answer
(C) **Jamaika ni ryokō shitara?** (E) How about a trip to Jamaica?	(C) **Sō suru koto ni shimashō.** (M) Yes, let's do that.
(P) **Yasui kippu ga arimasu ka?** (E) Can you give me a cheap ticket?	(C) **Ni-mai kaeba benkyō suru kamo shire nai.** (E) Buy two and I'll think about it.
(C) **Saikin kare wa hitozukiai ga waru-ku natta.** (E) Lately he has become unsociable.	(O) **Shokutaku de picha-picha shite shikarareru to sō naru.** (E) That's what happens if you're scolded for lip smacking at the table.
(O) **Anata ga kimochi o komenaide hanasu to, watashi wa dōsite yoika wakaranaku naru.** (E) When you speak without feeling I get upset.	(O) **Machidōshii kimochi o rikai suru.** (E) I understand your impatience.

Twist Your Tongue With These Tongue Twisters

6) **Hiyoko** (or, **kaeru) pyoko pyoko mipyoko pyoko awasete pyoko pyoko mupyoko pyoko. Nana pyoko ya pyoko koko no pyoko tō pyoko.**
The chicken (or, frog) jumped and jumped three times. Of the total the chicken jumped six times, jumped seven times, eight times, nine times and ten times jumped.

70 Basic Kana (な-Na) To (の-No) Stroke Order

Naguru zo!
I'll hit you!

Nagagutsu o haku.
I'm putting on long boots.

Nuginasai.
Undress.

Nusuma nai de.
Don't steal it.

Nemui.
I'm sleepy.

Nen-matsu wa isogashii.
I'm busy at the yearend.

Nintai nintai.
Be patient.

Nihon ni iku no mo yoshi ashi desu yo.
There are good and bad points about going to Japan.

Nokosu na!
Don't leave leftovers.

Nomasareru.
Forced me to drink.

FOUR STROKES

Today's Target Kana For Stroke Practice

Last Kana	Hiragana Soft Cursive Writing	Katakana Stiff Square Strokes	Next Kana
と	な	ナ	に
TO			NI

Hints For Stroke Order Reproduction And Recognition

(な-**na**), like 'na' in the name "Naomi", is the pronunciation of this kana. Avoid Kana Similarity Problems. Draw a loop at the bottom of the right side joint of this stroke since (た-**ta**) is almost horizontal at its base, and by being loopless it causes less problems of mistaken identity.

Target Strokes	1	2	3	4	5	6	7	8	9
な									
ナ	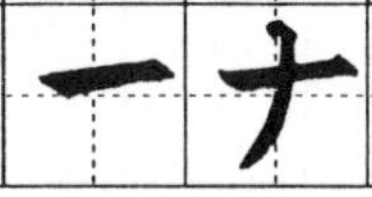								

Basic Kana (な-Na) To (の-No) Stroke Order

THREE STROKES

Today's Target Kana For Stroke Practice

Last Kana	Hiragana	Katakana	Next Kana
な	に	ニ	ぬ
NA	Hiragana Soft Cursive Writing	Katakana Stiff Square Strokes	NU

Hints For Stroke Order Reproduction And Recognition

(に-**ni**), which is similar to "knee", is the pronunciation sound for this kana. Avoid Kana Similarity Problems. These two kana look alike but the fact that one is hiragana and the other is katakana sets them apart even though their pronunciation is the same.

Target Strokes	1	2	3	4	5	6	7	8	9
に	㇐	㇐	に						
ニ	㇐	ニ							

TWO STROKES

Today's Target Kana For Stroke Practice

Last Kana	Hiragana Soft Cursive Writing	Katakana Stiff Square Strokes	Next Kana
に	ぬ	ヌ	ね
NI			NE

Hints For Stroke Order Reproduction And Recognition

(ぬ-**nu**), like the English word "new", is the pronunciation of this kana. Avoid Kana Similarity Problems. The left side of (ぬ-**nu**) sets it off from the vertical (ね-**ne**) which also has a loop formed at its base. (ぬ-**nu**) is looped at the bottom but a loop is missing from (め-**me**).

Target Strokes	1	2	3	4	5	6	7	8	9
ぬ		ぬ							
ヌ	フ	ヌ							

TWO STROKES

Today's Target Kana For Stroke Practice

Last Kana	Hiragana Soft Cursive Writing	Katakana Stiff Square Strokes	Next Kana
ぬ	ね	ネ	の
NU			NO

Hints For Stroke Order Reproduction And Recognition

(ね-**ne**), like the 'Ne' in the name "Ned", is the pronunciation of this kana. For the best stroke writing results, use a felt tip pen. Start from the left and follow the arrows. Using the very first kana as an example, slowly, with a light steady hand, try to accurately form your target kana. Use all the blank box spaces and imitate the strokes of your present and last kana until your kana resemble the original ones.

Target Strokes	1	2	3	4	5	6	7	8	9

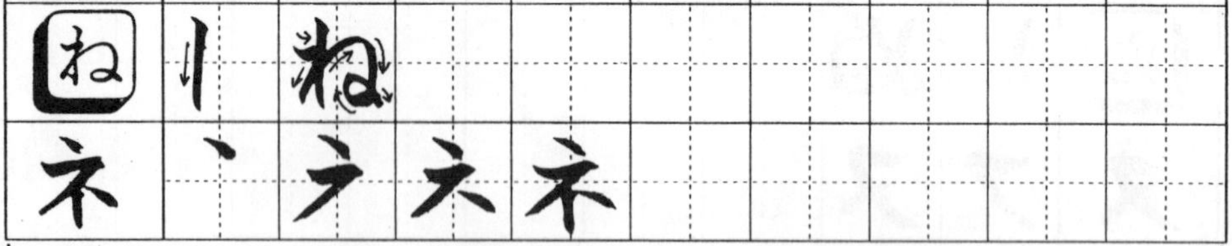

ONE STROKE

Today's Target Kana For Stroke Practice

Last Kana	Hiragana Soft Cursive Writing	Katakana Stiff Square Strokes	Next Kana
ね NE	の	ノ	は HA

Hints For Stroke Order Reproduction And Recognition

(の-**no**), like the English "No", is the pronunciation of this kana. For the best stroke writing results, use a felt tip pen. Then start from the left and follow the arrows. Using the very first kana as an example, slowly, with a light steady hand, try to accurately form your target kana. Use all the blank box spaces and imitate the strokes of your present and last kana until your kana resemble the original ones.

Target Strokes	1	2	3	4	5	6	7	8	9
の	の								
ノ	ノ								

Basic Kana (な-Na) To (の-No) Stroke Order

CREATIVE KANA REVIEW

Write it! Read it! Say it!

な	に	ぬ	ね	の
NA	NI	NU	NE	NO

LINK-A-LETTER: You have already practiced writing all the hiragana on this page. Now use them to build new words in the adjoining boxes. Then try to link them to phrases.

にく **niku** meat	ぬう **nuu** sew
なつ **natsu** summer	なに **nani** what
のこす **nokosu** leave	なか **naka** inside
あね **ane** sister	ないた **naita** cried
なし **nashi** pear	ない **nai** nothing

SEARCH AND MATCH IDENTICAL KANA

Expand your kana recognition ability. Search within the numbers (1-5) for the kana which matches the left hand column Romanized letters. Write the correct kana in the blank boxes. Then use the bottom page boxes to practice any kana you wish.

EXAMPLE:

		Answer	1	2	3	4	5
			↓	↓	↓	↓	↓
ga	←	3	だ	な	が	み	ぱ

Mark your correct answer numbers in these boxes below			1	2	3	4	5
		⬇	⬇	⬇	⬇	⬇	⬇
me	⬅		め	ね	ぬ	か	れ
a	⬅		あ	く	ば	ら	は
mi	⬅		け	う	さ	ふ	み
ma	⬅		や	る	ま	き	り
o	⬅		を	る	ぬ	り	ち

Practice writing any kana in these boxes

78 Vocabulary Expanding For Interacting

Temporal Clause Phrases

NATURAL SURVIVAL CONVERSATION

What You Might Hear	How You Might Possibly Answer
(C) **Shigoto no tsuide ni chotto yorimashita.** (E) I just dropped by to take care of some business.	(O) **Kono aida tegami o kaki nagara anata no koto o kangaeteita.** (E) The other day I was thinking about you while writing a letter.
(C) **Kinō wa sensei o yattsuke mashita ne.** (E) You put the teacher to shame yesterday.	(O) **Watashi o komarase yō to shita kara sore o shimashita.** (E) Yes, but only after he tried to embarrass me.
(C) **Rusu no aida ni yasui kirumono o tsukuraseta.** (E) I had some clothes made cheaply while I was out.	(O) **Honto ni kaimono ga jōzu desu ne.** (E) You're really good at finding bargains.
(O) **Kuraku nara nai uchi ni kaeranakucha.** (E) I'd better leave before it gets dark.	(O) **Anata ga dete iru uchi ni apāto o sōji shimashō.** (E) While you are out I'll clean the apartment.
(C) **Anata ga kuru mae wa taihen kitanakatta.** (M) Before you came it was really untidy.	(O) **Natsu no uchi wa hiru mo yoru mo mado o akete okimasu.** (E) During the summer I leave my windows open day and night.
(O) **Sanzoku no kutsushita shika motte inai.** (E) I only have three pairs of socks.	(O) **Hajimete shigoto o hajimeta toki issoku no kutsushita shika motte nakatta.** (E) When I started on my first job I only had one pair of socks.
(O) **Ooki na mushi ga tobikonde kuru tabi ni mado o shimeta.** (E) I shut the window every time big bugs flew in.	(C) **Denwa ryōkin o haratte iru aida ni abazure ga chikazuite kuru no o mita.** (M) While paying my phone bill a shameless hussey approached me.
(O) **Tenshi no yō ni furumaitai toki ni akuma ga deru.** (E) Sometimes when you want to act like an angel, devils always appear.	(O) **Yokereba hachiji made itemo ii desu.** (E) Stay here until eight if you like.

NATURAL SURVIVAL CONVERSATION

What You Might Hear	How You Might Possibly Answer
(C) **Tsumetaku naru mae ni kore o tabete.** (W) Eat this before it gets cold.	(O) **Sonna ni kūhuku dewa nai.** (M) I'm not very hungry.
(O) **Shuppatsu mae ni denwa o kanarazu kakeru yō ni.** (E) Be sure to call me before you depart.	(O) **Ryokō-chū ni ehagaki o okurimasu.** (E) I'll send you a picture postcard during my trip.
(C) **Asa gohan o tabete iru aida shigoto ni deruki ga nakunatta.** (M) While eating breakfast I suddenly didn't feel like showing up for work.	(O) **Shikashi kikaku o goji made ni owaraseru yakusoku shita.** (E) But you promised to finish the plan by 5 o'clock.
(O) **Kare ga tabako o sutte iru aida wa watashi no ken-enken wa shingai sareta.** (E) He's violating my non-smoker's rights while he's smoking that smelly cigarette.	(O) **Kare wa omoi yari no nai hito da. Kare wa tanin o ira-ira saseru beki dewa nai.** (E) He's such an inconsiderate person. He should stop irritating people.

Twist Your Tongue With These Tongue Twisters

9) **Kanda Kaji-cho no kado no kambutsuya de katsuobushi o katte katakute kame nai kaeshite kaero.**
I brought dried bonito in a dry provisions shop on Kaji Street corner in Kanda. It was so hard I could hardly chew it so I returned it and now I returned home.

80 Basic Kana (は-Ha) To (ほ-Ho) Stroke Order

Hagaki o kaiteiru.
I'm writing a post-card.

Ha o migaita.
I brushed my teeth.

Hi ga nobotte iru.
The sun is rising.

Hima ga nai.
I have no time.

Hima tsubushi ni wa totemo yoi desu yo.
It's a really good way to kill time.

Nani ka yoi hima tsubushi wa nai deshōka?
Do you know any good ways for me to kill time?

Fue o fukinasai.
Blow your whistle.

Futotte iru.
Is fat.

Samui shi, ame mo futte iru, ikitaku nai.
It's cold and rain-ing.
go.

Heiki desu.
It's alright.

Henji o shimasu.
I'll give you an answer.

Hon mono desu.
It's genuine.

Hōki de haita.
I swept with a broom.

THREE STROKES

Today's Target Kana For Stroke Practice

Last Kana			Next Kana
の	は	ハ	ひ
NO	Hiragana Soft Cursive Writing	Katakana Stiff Square Strokes	HI

Hints For Stroke Order Reproduction And Recognition

(は-**ha**) is the pronunciation of this kana. The 'h' is given a much weaker sound than the 'h' in, for example, such English words as "home" or "hat". Avoid Kana Similarity Problems. (は-**ha**) is drawn with one horizontal stroke while (ほ **ho**) receives two horizontal strokes. For the best stroke writing results, use a felt tip pen. Start from the left and follow the arrows. Using the very first kana as an example, slowly, with a light steady hand, try to accurately form your target kana. Use all the blank box spaces and imitate the strokes of your present and last kana until your kana resemble the original ones.

Target Strokes	1	2	3	4	5	6	7	8	9
は									
ハ									

Basic Kana (は-Ha) To (ほ-Ho) Stroke Order

ONE STROKE

Today's Target Kana For Stroke Practice

Last Kana			Next Kana
は	ひ	ヒ	ふ
HA	Hiragana Soft Cursive Writing	Katakana Stiff Square Strokes	FU

Hints For Stroke Order Reproduction And Recognition

(ひ-**hi**), which sounds like the English word "he", is the pronunciation of this kana. However, the 'h' before an 'i' is pronounced by positioning your tongue close to the roof of your mouth and producing a friction sound similar to the 'ch' in the German word "ich".

Target Strokes	1	2	3	4	5	6	7	8	9
ひ	ひ								
ヒ	ノ	ヒ							

FOUR STROKES

Today's Target Kana For Stroke Practice

Last Kana	Hiragana Soft Cursive Writing	Katakana Stiff Square Strokes	Next Kana
ひ	ふ	フ	へ
HI			HE

Hints For Stroke Order Reproduction And Recognition

(**ふ-fu**), which sounds like the 'fu' of the English word "full", is the pronunciation of this kana. It is made by bringing your two unrounded lips together as if blowing out candles while producing sound. Your teeth do not touch your lips as when saying "funny" or "funky."

Target Strokes	1	2	3	4	5	6	7	8	9
ふ	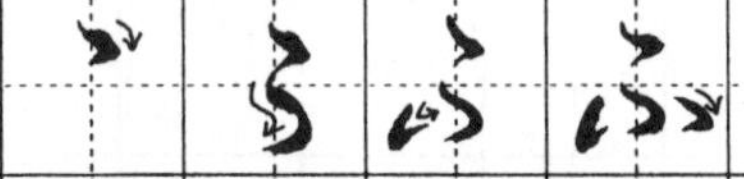								
フ	フ								

ONE STROKE

Today's Target Kana For Stroke Practice

Last Kana			Next Kana
ふ	へ	ヘ	ほ
FU	Hiragana Soft Cursive Writing	Katakana Stiff Square Strokes	HO

Hints For Stroke Order Reproduction And Recognition

(へ-**he**), which sounds like the 'he' in the English word "heather", is the pronunciation of this kana. Avoid Kana Similarity Problems. These two kana are very similar in appearance and identical in pronunciation. What sets them apart is that one is hiragana and the other is katakana.

Target Strokes	1	2	3	4	5	6	7	8	9
へ	へ								
ヘ	ヘ								

FOUR STROKES

Today's Target Kana For Stroke Practice

Last Kana	Hiragana Soft Cursive Writing	Katakana Stiff Square Strokes	Next Kana
へ	ほ	ホ	ま
HE			MA

Hints For Stroke Order Reproduction And Recognition

(**ほ-ho**) , which sounds like the Santa Claus' greeting "ho ho ho", is the pronunciation of this kana. For the best stroke writing results, use a felt tip pen. Start from the left and follow the arrows. Using the very first kana as an example, slowly, with a light steady hand, try to accurately form your target kana. Use all the blank box spaces and imitate the strokes of your present and last kana until your kana resemble the original ones.

Target Strokes	1	2	3	4	5	6	7	8	9
ほ				ほ					
ホ	一	十	才	ホ					

Basic Kana (は-Ha) To (ほ-Ho) Stroke Order

CREATIVE KANA REVIEW

Write it! Read it! Say it!

は	ひ	ふ	へ	ほ
HA	HI	FU	HE	HO

LINK-A-LETTER: You have already practiced writing all the hiragana on this page. Now use them to build new words in the adjoining boxes. Then try to link them to phrases.

はい **hai** yes	はこ **hako** a box
はく **haku** put on shoes	ふね **fune** a boat
ひく **hiku** pull open	は **ha** teeth
ひと **hito** a person	へた **heta** not good at
ふく **fuku** wipe	はな **hana** flower

NATURAL SURVIVAL CONVERSATION

What You Might Hear	How You Might Possibly Answer
(O) **Kare wa isogashii to itta.** (E) He said he's busy.	(C) **Kare dake janakute minna isogashii to yutte kure.** (E) Tell him everybody's busy, not just him.
(P) **Nihon ni tsuite no shitsumon ni taisuru kare no hannō wa dō deshita ka?** (E) What was his reaction to your question about Japan?	(O) **Nihon wa fukeiki ka to kare ni kiitara sō da to kotaeta.** (E) When I asked him if Japan is in recession he replied "definitely".
(P) **Daiyosan no yōkyū ni kanshite kare wa do no yō ni kotaemashita ka?** (E) How did he respond to your request for a larger budget?	(O) **Kare wa motto yosan ga hitsuyō dato setsumei shita.** (E) He explained that he needed more details.
(O) **Henna gaijin to kare wa tsubuyaita.** (E) He muttered "weird foreigner".	(P) **Shōganai.** (E) It can't be helped.
(P) **Kare wa dōshite sonna ni akaku nattano desu ka?** (E) What made him look so red faced?	(P) **Kare ni hanakuso hojiri wa warui to omoimasu to itta kara.** (E) I told him that I thought nose-picking was disgusting.
(C) **Kare wa jibun de menkui dato itta.** (E) He told me that he only likes beautiful women.	(P) **Keredomo kanojotachi wa kare o dō omoimasu ka?** (E) But how do the women feel about him?

88 Basic Kana (ま-Ma) To (も-Mo) Stroke Order

Maigo ni natta.
I lost my child.

Machi kutabireru.
I'm tired of waiting.

Ato gofun dake matte kudasai.
Please wait just five minutes more.

Misuborashii desu.
He's shabby.

Mite kudasai.
Please take a look.

Dekiru ka dō ka tonikaku yatte mimashō.
At any rate, I will do whatever I can.

Tamanegi o mukinasai.
Peel the onions.

Muneyake ga suru.
I have heartburn.

Mukai ni iku.
I'll go meet you.

Megane o kakeru.
I wear glasses.

Meshi agatte kudasai.
Please eat.

Momi-hogushite kudasai.
Please massage me.

Mō sukoshi kudasai.
A little more please.

THREE STROKES

Today's Target Kana For Stroke Practice

Last Kana	ま	マ	Next Kana
ほ	Hiragana Soft Cursive Writing	Katakana Stiff Square Strokes	み
HO			MI

Hints For Stroke Order Reproduction And Recognition

(ま-**ma**), which sounds like the 'ma' in the English word "marvelous", is the pronunciation of this kana. Avoid Kana Similarity Problems. The kana (ま-ma) is drawn with a loop at its base, while (も-**mo**) ends with an upswept stem. Notice that the base of (ま-**ma**) has two horizontal strokes while (よ-**yo**) has only one short right side horizontal stroke on its vertical form.

Target Strokes	1	2	3	4	5	6	7	8	9
ま	一	二	ま						
マ	フ	マ							

TWO STROKES

Today's Target Kana For Stroke Practice

Last Kana	Hiragana Soft Cursive Writing	Katakana Stiff Square Strokes	Next Kana
ま	み	ミ	む
MA			MU

Hints For Stroke Order Reproduction And Recognition

(み-**mi**), which sounds like the 'Mi' of "Mickey", is the pronunciation of this kana. For the best stroke writing results, use a felt tip pen. Start from the left and follow the arrows. Using the very first kana as an example, slowly, with a light steady hand, try to accurately form your target kana. Use all the blank box spaces and imitate the strokes of your present and last kana until your kana resemble the original ones.

Target Strokes	1	2	3	4	5	6	7	8	9
み	み	み							
ミ			ミ						

THREE STROKES

Today's Target Kana For Stroke Practice

Last Kana	Hiragana Soft Cursive Writing	Katakana Stiff Square Strokes	Next Kana
み	む	ム	め
MI			ME

Hints For Stroke Order Reproduction And Recognition

(む-**mu**), which sounds like the 'mo' of "movie", is the pronunciation of this kana. For the best stroke writing results, use a felt tip pen. Start from the left and follow the arrows. Using the very first kana as an example, slowly, with a light steady hand, try to accurately form your target kana. Use all the blank box spaces and imitate the strokes of your present and last kana until your kana resemble the original ones.

Target Strokes	1	2	3	4	5	6	7	8	9
む	一	む	む						
ム	㇜	ム							

TWO STROKES

Today's Target Kana For Stroke Practice

Last Kana	Hiragana Soft Cursive Writing	Katakana Stiff Square Strokes	Next Kana
む	め	メ	も
MU			MO

Hints For Stroke Order Reproduction And Recognition

(め-**me**), which sounds like the 'me' of "mend", is the pronunciation of this kana. For the best stroke writing results, use a felt tip pen. Start from the left and follow the arrows. Using the very first kana as an example, slowly, with a light steady hand, try to accurately form your target kana. Use all the blank box spaces and imitate the strokes of your present and last kana until your kana resemble the original ones.

Target Strokes	1	2	3	4	5	6	7	8	9
め		め							
メ		メ							

THREE STROKES

Today's Target Kana For Stroke Practice

Last Kana	Hiragana Soft Cursive Writing	Katakana Stiff Square Strokes	Next Kana
め ME	も	モ	や YA

Hints For Stroke Order Reproduction And Recognition

(も-**mo**), which sounds like the 'mo' of "mosaic", is the pronunciation of this kana. Avoid Kana Similarity Problems. These two kana are similar in appearance and have the same pronunciation. But remember, one is hiragana and the other is katakana.

Target Strokes	1	2	3	4	5	6	7	8	9
も	し	t	も						
モ	一	二	モ						

CREATIVE KANA REVIEW

Write it! Read it! Say it!

ま	み	む	め	も
MA	MI	MU	ME	MO

LINK-A-LETTER: You have already practiced writing all the hiragana on this page. Now use them to build new words in the adjoining boxes. Then try to link them to phrases.

まけ **make** defeat				もしもし **moshimoshi** hello			
みち **michi** road				みせ **mise** store			
まさか **masaka** surely not				むかえ **mukae** meet someone			
むりょう **muryō** free				め **me** eyes			
もつ **motsu** bring				むし **mushi** insect			

(Point Out What's Wrong)

Remembering what you have already read regarding stroke order, carefully notice how these strokes are written. See how you measure up.

This kana → ば is the correct stroke for → ば

Notice how the correct stroke begins and ends. Now check and see what you may have done wrong, check one box with an 'X'.

This stroke み is wrong because it was written

Above the line	Below the line	It's okay
☐	☐	☐

This stroke え is wrong because it was drawn

Too short	Too long	It's okay
☐	☐	☐

The correct stroke line goes upwards 

To the right	To the left	It's okay
☐	☐	☐

Put a check mark below each wrongly stroked kana and write the correct way it should appear in the spare boxes and pronounce each kana aloud with your Japanese 'kana helpmate'.

Review strokes →	ぴ	ぎゅ	む	よ
Your stroke →				

96 Vocabulary Expanding For Interacting

Negative Sentences

NATURAL SURVIVAL CONVERSATION

What You Might Hear	How You Might Possibly Answer
(P) **Hiragana ga kakemasu ka?** (E) Can you write hiragana?	(P) **Osoraku renshū sureba kakeru deshō.** (E) I probably could write it if I practiced.
(P) **Hito o warawasu koto ga dekimasu ka?** (E) Can you make people laugh?	(P) **Sō naru deshō.** (E) It's just possible.
(O) **Taberaremasu ka?** (E) Can I eat this?	(P) **Hai. Shokuchūdoku ni wa naranai deshō.** (E) Yes, you won't get food poisoning.
(P) **Ryōri ga dekimasu ka?** (E) Can you cook?	(P) **Moshi tsuma ga daidokoro ni inakereba tameseru deshō.** (M) I only try if my wife isn't in the kitchen.
(O) **Kare wa mukuchi da.** (E) He doesn't talk much.	(P) **Uchiki dakara deshō.** (E) He's probably shy.
(P) **Sono jōhō o dō yatte shitta no desu ka?** (E) How did you find that information?	(O) **Yūjin kara kuchikomi de oshiete moratta.** (E) By word of mouth from my friend.
(O) **Kare wa hanzai o okasu keikō ga aru rashii.** (E) He seems to have criminal tendencies.	(C) **Sonna hazu wa nai.** (E) That can't be true.
(P) **Aikawarazu kare no ie wa tabun yogoreno nai jōtai deshō.** (E) His house is probably in immaculate condition as always.	(P) **Sō deshō.** (E) Yes, that's probably so.
(O) **Anata wa yakkai mono no yō ni mieru.** (E) You look like a trouble maker.	(P) **Anata wa namaiki de jibun no hi o mitomenai deshō.** (E) You're sassy and you won't admit you're wrong.

NATURAL SURVIVAL CONVERSATION

What You Might Hear	How You Might Possibly Answer
(O) **Watashi wa itsumo sore ga dekina-katta.** (E) I have never been able to do that.	(P) **Osoraku anata wa jishin ga na-katta no deshō.** (E) Probably because you lack confi-dence.
(P) **Yakusoku wa kanarazu mamo-rimasu.** (E) I will keep my promise absolutely.	(O) **Sō dato iin desu kedo.** (W) That will be good.
(P) **Shiawase ga kuru deshō.** (E) Happiness can be achieved.	(O) **Sō kamo shirenai.** (E) That may be so.
(P) **Kyō wa furusato ni kaerimasu ka ?** (E) Will you go to your hometown today ?	(P) **Ima kara shuppatsu suru tsumori desu.** (E) I intend to start out for it now.
(P) **Dare ka ni butsukatta toki dō-shimasu ka ?** (E) When you accidentaly bump someone, what should you do ?	(P) **Ayamaru beki desu.** (E) I should apologize.

Twist Your Tongue With These Tongue Twisters

8) **Ka ga, ka ka, ga ga ka ka, dochira kana ga ka ka ?**
Mosquito or moth, moth or mosquito, I wonder if it's a moth or a mosquito ? (author's original)

9) **Kono en no shita no kugi chotto hikinuki nikui kugi.**
It's too difficult to pull out the nail from under the base of the floor.

10) **Kono kugi wa hikinuki nikui kugi.**
This nail could not be pulled out easily.

98 Basic Kana (や-Ya) To (よ-Yo) Stroke Order

Yarinasai! Do it!

Yari yasui. It's easy to do.

Yari nikui. It's hard to do.

Yakusoku o mamore.
Keep your word.

Kayōbi wa yasumi.
Tuesday is my day off.

Watashi wa yaruki ga nai.
I don't feel like doing it.

O yu o kudasai.
Please give me some hot water.

Yurushite kudasai.
Please forgive me.

Fuzai yūbinbutsu o tori ni kimashita.
I'd like to pick up the mail kept here while I was absent.

Yōkoso.
Welcome.

Yorokonde ikimasu.
I'm happy to go.

Yowaki o dashite wa ikemasen.
Have courage and hang in there!

THREE STROKES

Today's Target Kana For Stroke Practice

Last Kana			Next Kana
も	や	ヤ	ゆ
MO	Hiragana Soft Cursive Writing	Katakana Stiff Square Strokes	YU

Hints For Stroke Order Reproduction And Recognition

(や-**ya**), which sounds like the 'ya' in the English word "yams", is the pronunciation of this kana. Avoid Kana Similarity Problems. These two kana look alike but one is hiragana and the other katakana, which sets them apart even though they have the same pronunciation.

Target Strokes	1	2	3	4	5	6	7	8	9

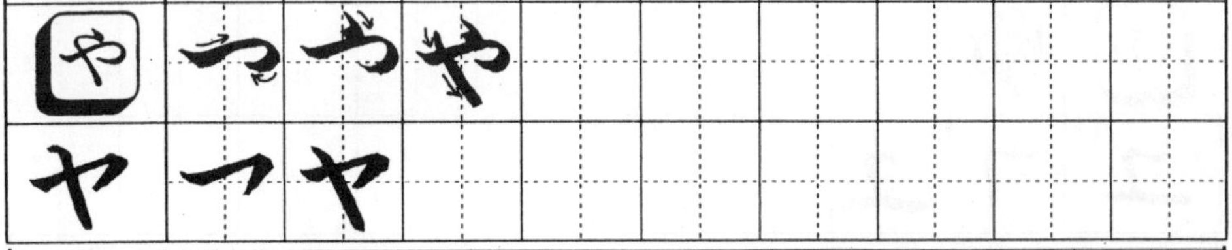

Basic Kana (や-Ya) To (よ-Yo) Stroke Order

ONE STROKE

Today's Target Kana For Stroke Practice

Last Kana	Hiragana Soft Cursive Writing	Katakana Stiff Square Strokes	Next Kana
や	ゆ	ユ	よ
YA			YO

Hints For Stroke Order Reproduction And Recognition

(ゆ-**yu**), which sounds exactly like the English word "you", is the pronunciation of this kana. For the best stroke writing results, use a felt tip pen. Start from the left and follow the arrows. Using the very first kana as an example, slowly, with a light steady hand, try to accurately form your target kana. Use all the blank box spaces and imitate the strokes of your present and last kana until your kana resemble the original ones.

Target Strokes	1	2	3	4	5	6	7	8	9
ゆ	ゆ								
ユ	フ	ユ							

TWO STROKES

Today's Target Kana For Stroke Practice

Last Kana			Next Kana
ゆ	よ	ヨ	ら
YU	Hiragana Soft Cursive Writing	Katakana Stiff Square Strokes	RA

Hints For Stroke Order Reproduction And Recognition

(よ-**yo**), which sounds like the 'yo' of "New York", is the pronunciation of this kana. For the best stroke writing results, use a felt tip pen. Start from the left and follow the arrows. Using the very first kana as an example, slowly, with a light steady hand, try to accurately form your target kana. Use all the blank box spaces and imitate the strokes of your present and last kana until your kana resemble the original ones.

Target Strokes	1	2	3	4	5	6	7	8	9
よ	⼀	よ							
ヨ	フ	ヲ	ヨ						

Basic Kana (や-Ya) To (よ-Yo) Stroke Order

CREATIVE KANA REVIEW

Write it! Read it! Say it!

や		ゆ		よ
YA		YU		YO

LINK-A-LETTER: You have already practiced writing all the hiragana on this page. Now use them to build new words in the adjoining boxes. Then try to link them to phrases.

やくそく **yakusoku** make a promise				ゆき **yuki** snow		
やすみ **yasumi** rest, period				よもや **yomoya** surely not		
よく **yoku** often				ようやく **yōyaku** at last		
やさしい **yasashii** kind				やすもの **yasumono** cheap goods		
ゆううつ **yūutsu** depressed				よい **yoi** good		

SEARCH AND MATCH IDENTICAL KANA

Expand your kana recognition ability. Search within the numbers (1-5) for the kana which matches the left hand column Romanized letters. Write the correct kana in the blank boxes. Then use the bottom page boxes to practice any kana you wish.

EXAMPLE:

Answer

			1	2	3	4	5
			↓	↓	↓	↓	↓
ga	←	3	だ	な	が	み	ぱ

	Mark your correct answer numbers in these boxes below		1	2	3	4	5
		⬇	⬇	⬇	⬇	⬇	⬇
bu	⬅		ぞ	べ	び	ば	ぶ
jo	⬅		じゅ	びょ	じょ	ちゃ	ぎょ
kyu	⬅		きゃ	しゃ	きゅ	しゅ	きょ
bi	⬅		じ	ず	ぶ	ば	び
pu	⬅		ぴょ	ひょ	ぶ	ぷ	ぺ

Practice writing any kana in these boxes

104

Vocabulary Expanding For Interacting

Special Use of Interrogative Pronouns

NATURAL SURVIVAL CONVERSATION

What You Might Hear	How You Might Possibly Answer
(P) **Chikagoro wa ikaga desu ka?** (E) How have you been lately?	(P) **Zutto gairai kanja de imasu.** (E) I am an outpatient at the local hospital.
(C) **Osoku tsuita node dare mo inakunatta to iwareta.** (E) I arrived late and was told that everybody had gone.	(P) **Minna doko e ikimashita ka?** (E) Where did they all go?
(P) **Anata no apāto ni kare o shōtai suru koto o kangaete imasu ka?** (E) Are you thinking of inviting him to your apartment?	(O) **Iie ano hito wa itsu mo kimasen.** (E) No, he never shows up.
(C) **Namben mo kiita no ni wakatte kure nai.** (E) Though he listened to me many times he still couldn't understand.	(P) **Kyōiku dekinai hito mo iru no desu ne.** (E) Don't you think that some people are just uneducatable?
(O) **Kono machi ni hajimete kimashita no wa itsu desu ka?** (E) When did you first come to this town?	(O) **Oboeterarenai hodo mukashi desu.** (E) More years ago than I care to remember.
(P) **Kono kinjo wa seikatsu shi yasui desu ka?** (E) Is it easy to live in this neighborhood?	(O) **Iie, kinjo ni sensakuzuki na rinjin ga ōi desu.** (E) No, because there's a lot of nosey neighbors.
(P) **Kinō yori kyō wa hito ga ōi.** (E) There's a lot more people out today than yesterday.	(P) **Takusan no hito o mita koto go nai no desu ka?** (E) Haven't you ever seen a lot of people before?
(P) **Watashitachi no machi wa dō desu ka?** (E) How do you like our town?	(O) **Asa no kono machi ga ichiban suki desu.** (E) I like it best in the morning.

NATURAL SURVIVAL CONVERSATION

What You Might Hear	How You Might Possibly Answer
(C) **Ritsuko-chan wa donna ko desu ka? Futotte imasu ka? Yasete imasu ka?** (E) How does Ms. Ritsuko look? Is she fat or skinny?	(O) **Dō hyōgen shite iika wakaranai.** (*or*) Nanto mo iiyō ga nai. (*this last line is funny*) (E) She's beyond description!
(W) **Anta ano ko no nan na nosa?** (M) What are you to her?	(M) **Fushigina en de bokutachi wa de-atta.** (M) We met by a strange coincidence.
(O) **Kanojo to wa shitashii desu ka?** (E) Is your relationship with her close?	(O) **Dōkyo suru yō ni narimashita.** (E) We live together.
(O) **Nani yo? Watashi mise mono ja nai yo!** (W) What are you staring at?	(P) **Anata o ai shite imasu.** (E) I love you!
(C) **Naze ano hito ga erabaretan deshō?** (E) Why was that person chosen?	(O) **Minna kubi o hinette imasu yo.** (E) Everyone's racking their brains for the answer.

Twist Your Tongue With These Tongue Twisters

11) **Kimi miru sono kimi wa kimi no kimi.**
The yolk of the egg which you see is your yolk.

12) **Kono tatekake ni take tatekake tano wa take tatekake takatta kara take tatekaketa.**
The reason why I hang this bamboo on the wall is because I want to hang it on the wall.

13) **Nitta wa niyaniya ninjin motte Niigata kara nigeta.**
With a smile on his face and a carrot in his hand, Nitta escaped from Niigata (Prefecture).

106 Basic Kana (ら-Ra) To (ろ-Ro) Stroke Order

Ranbō mono.
A tough guy.

Rakugaki o suru.
Scribbling graffiti.

Rikai shimasu.
I understand.

Risō no hito.
An ideal person.

Renraku shimasu.
I'll be in touch.

Reigi o shiranai.
Doesn't know etiquette.

Rusu ni suru.
Is out.

Runpen ga iru.
He's a tramp.

Rokuon suru.
To record.

Rōka o hashiru na.
Don't run in the hallway.

TWO STROKES

Today's Target Kana For Stroke Practice

Last Kana			Next Kana
よ	ら	ラ	り
YO	Hiragana Soft Cursive Writing	Katakana Stiff Square Strokes	RI

Hints For Stroke Order Reproduction And Recognition

(ら-**ra**), which sounds like the 'ra' of the Indian title "raj", is the pronunciation of this kana. A Japanese 'r' sound is made by letting the tongue flick hard up against the back of your upper front teeth. Avoid Kana Similarity Problems. The initial (ら-**ra**) stroke is written small with a slight slant, detached from the vertical second stroke, which is rounded at its base. Take care not to make the top of the vertical form too short or it may be mistaken for (う-**u**) . Though these two kana look alike, remember, one is hiragana while the other is katakana. The top of the katakana (ラ-**ra**) is a single horizontal non-connecting stroke above the second stroke, but the katakana (ヲ-**o**) has two top connected horizontal strokes.

Target Strokes	1	2	3	4	5	6	7	8	9
ら	`	ら							
ラ	一	ラ							

TWO STROKES

Today's Target Kana For Stroke Practice

Last Kana	Hiragana Soft Cursive Writing	Katakana Stiff Square Strokes	Next Kana
ら	り	リ	る
RA			RU

Hints For Stroke Order Reproduction And Recognition

(り-**ri**), which sounds like the 're' in the name "Reeves", is the pronunciation of this kana. Avoid Kana Similarity Problems. The big difference between these two kana, which are similar in sound and appearance is that one is hiragana while the other is katakana.

Target Strokes	1	2	3	4	5	6	7	8	9
り									
リ									

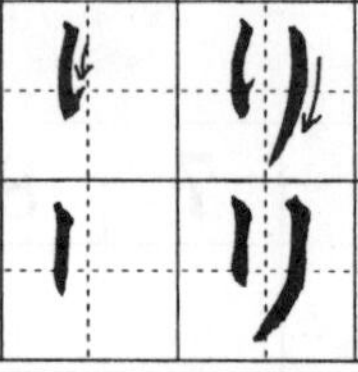

ONE STROKE

Today's Target Kana For Stroke Practice

Last Kana			Next Kana
り	る	ル	れ
RI	Hiragana Soft Cursive Writing	Katakana Stiff Square Strokes	RE

Hints For Stroke Order Reproduction And Recognition

(る-**ru**), which sounds like the 'ru' of "ruby", is the pronunciation sound of this kana. Avoid Kana Similarity Problems. The big difference between the kana (る-**ru**) and the kana (ろ-**ro**) is that (る-**ru**) is drawn with a loop whereas (ろ-**ro**) is loopless.

Target Strokes	1	2	3	4	5	6	7	8	9
る	る								
ル	ノ	ル							

TWO STROKES

Today's Target Kana For Stroke Practice

Last Kana	Hiragana Soft Cursive Writing	Katakana Stiff Square Strokes	Next Kana
る	れ	レ	ろ
RU			RO

Hints For Stroke Order Reproduction And Recognition

(**れ-re**), which sounds like the 're' in "reverend", is the pronunciation of this kana. Avoid Kana Similarity Problems. The final stroke of (**れ-re**) slides downward and then curves slightly upward towards the right but the final stroke of (**わ-wa**) is rounded and curved inward to the left.

Target Strokes	1	2	3	4	5	6	7	8	9
れ	丨	れ							
レ	レ								

ONE STROKE

Today's Target Kana For Stroke Practice

Last Kana			Next Kana
れ	ろ	ロ	わ
RE	Hiragana Soft Cursive Writing	Katakana Stiff Square Strokes	WA

Hints For Stroke Order Reproduction And Recognition

(ろ-**ro**), which sounds like the 'ro' in "robot", is the pronunciation of this kana. For the best stroke writing results, use a felt tip pen. Start from the left and follow the arrows. Using the very first kana as an example, slowly, with a light steady hand, try to accurately form your target kana. Use all the blank box spaces and imitate the strokes of your present and last kana until your kana resemble the original ones.

Target Strokes	1	2	3	4	5	6	7	8	9
ろ									
ロ									

Basic Kana (ら-Ra) To (ろ-Ro) Stroke Order

CREATIVE KANA REVIEW

Write it! Read it! Say it!

ら	り	る	れ	ろ
RA	RI	RU	RE	RO

LINK-A-LETTER: You have already practiced writing all the hiragana on this page. Now use them to build new words in the adjoining boxes. Then try to link them to phrases.

るす **rusu** to be out				りこうな **rikō na** clever			
らしい **rashii** it seems				ろく **roku** six			
るい **rui** kind, sort				りかい **rikai** understanding			
れい **rei** to bow				ろうそく **rōsoku** candle			
らくな **raku na** easy				れいぎ **reigi** manners			

SEARCH AND MATCH IDENTICAL KANA 113

Expand your kana recognition ability. Search within the numbers (1-5) for the kana which matches the left hand column Romanized letters. Write the correct kana in the blank boxes. Then use the bottom page boxes to practice any kana you wish.

EXAMPLE :

Answer

			1	2	3	4	5
			↓	↓	↓	↓	↓
ga	←	3	だ	な	が	み	ぱ

Mark your correct answer numbers in these boxes below			1	2	3	4	5
		⬇	⬇	⬇	⬇	⬇	⬇
re	⬅		れ	ら	あ	ぜ	ほ
i	⬅		た	て	い	ら	ど
yo	⬅		こ	よ	ざ	ぎ	る
to	⬅		の	べ	きよ	じゃ	と
mi	⬅		ふぁ	み	く	こ	つ

Practice writing any kana in these boxes

Vocabulary Expanding For Interacting

Examples of Negative Form Sentences

NATURAL SURVIVAL CONVERSATION

What You Might Hear	How You Might Possibly Answer
(P) **Musuko no sei de haji o kakasareta.** (E) We have been shamed thanks to our son.	(O) **Kandō shinasai!** (E) Disown him!
(C) **Sonna koto o shinai yō ni shite kudasai.** (E) Please don't do that sort of thing.	(O) **Yatte shimatta koto wa shikata ga nai.** (E) What's done is done.
(P) **Dekiru ka dō ka?** (E) Can it be done or not?	(O) **Dekiru ka dō ka wakaranai.** (E) I don't know if it can be done or not.
(P) **Jikan ga nai no de isogimashō.** (E) I'm short of time so let's hurry!	(O) **Sonna hanashi kata wa yame nasai.** (E) Don't talk like that.
(C) **Kore wa jōdan da.** (E) This is a joke.	(P) **Anata wa omoshiroku nai.** (E) You're not an interesting person.
(C) **Konna hon wa yomanai.** (E) I don't read this kind of book.	(C) **Boku no dewa nai.** (M) It's not mine.
(P) **Oda-san dewa arimasen ka?** (E) You are Mr. Oda aren't you?	(O) **Mattaku chigaimasu.** (E) You're absolutely wrong.
(P) **Kinō byōki de shigoto ni ikemasen deshita.** (E) I didn't go to work yesterday because I was sick.	(O) **Byōki ni naru nowa tayasui.** (E) It's easy to get sick.
(P) **Nokotte iru mono ga arimasen.** (E) There isn't anything left.	(C) **Mō sukoshi chūmon shitara.** (E) Why don't you order some more?
(P) **Kono aida minna no mae de haji o kakasaremashita.** (E) I was put to shame the other day, in front of everyone.	(C) **Morashita no?** (E) Did you wet your pants?

NATURAL SURVIVAL CONVERSATION

What You Might Hear	How You Might Possibly Answer
(O) **Hanako wa chikaku no hiroba ni aru ōkina ōkina funsui de matte iru.** (E) Hanako is waiting near the huge fountain in the plaza.	(O) **Shikashi kanojo no kakushi-go no ie wa chikaku ni nai.** (E) But her secret child's house is not around here.

Twist Your Tongue With These Tongue Twisters

14) **Nama mugi namagome nama tamago.**
Unproccesed rice, unprocessed wheat and raw eggs.

15) **Oyagame no ue ni kogame, kogame no ue ni magogame magogame no ue ni himagogame.**
The grandchild turtle is on top of the child turtle and the children turtle are on top of the parent turtle.

16) **Okashiya-san, okamiya-san, Okamoto-san, sono okyaku-san no naka de dore ga okama-chan ?**
Among these three customers, the baker, the paper-seller and Mr. Okamoto, which one is gay ? (original)

17) **Nozoki mi suru toki wa me o akikitte nozoki miyo !**
A peeping Tom's eyes beam with delight when he sees what he wants to see. (original)

18) **Shinshun shinjin shanson shō.**
New Year's new singers' French song show.

116 Basic Kana (わ-Wa) To (ん-Un) Stroke Order

Wairo A bribe

Wakari yasui desu.
It's easy to understand.

Anata wa wasureppoi.
You are forgetful.

Wagamama na hito.
A selfish person.

Kare wa wazato yatta.
He did it on purpose.

Anata o aishite iru.
I love you.

Hana o hojiru na!
Don't pick your nose!

Kyūryō o agenai to norou zo!
If my salary isn't raised I'll put a curse on you!

Un.
Yes.

Unsō gaisha de hataraite iru.
I work in a moving company.

TWO STROKES

Today's Target Kana For Stroke Practice

Last Kana	Hiragana Soft Cursive Writing	Katakana Stiff Square Strokes	Next Kana
ろ	わ	ワ	を
RO			O

Hints For Stroke Order Reproduction And Recognition

(わ-**wa**), which sounds like the 'wa' in "wander", is the pronunciation of this kana. While pronouncing 'wa' in Japanese your lips must be more relaxed than in when saying the English 'wa'. Avoid Kana Similarity Problems. Although the left side of these two kana, (わ-**wa**) and (ね-**ne**) are drawn the same, the base of 'wa' is loopless while the base of '**ne**' is looped. The first stroke of the katakana (ワ-**wa**) is short, followed by a long connecting horizontal stroke which slides from a vertical to a curved form. However, the first stroke of the katakana (ク-**ku**) is short and curved. It has a short horizontal stroke and a vertical stroke which is curved to the left at the base.

Target Strokes	1	2	3	4	5	6	7	8	9
わ	丨	わ							
ワ	丶	ワ							

THREE STROKES

Today's Target Kana For Stroke Practice

Last Kana	Hiragana Soft Cursive Writing	Katakana Stiff Square Strokes	Next Kana
わ	を	ヲ	ん
WA			UN

Hints For Stroke Order Reproduction And Recognition

(を-**o**), which sounds like the surprise word "oh", is the pronunciation of this kana, which is used strictly as a particle and does not form part of any word in Japanese grammar. Avoid Kana Similarity Problems. You've seen these two kana earlier. Though similar in appearance, remember, one is hiragana and the other is katakana.

Target Strokes	1	2	3	4	5	6	7	8	9

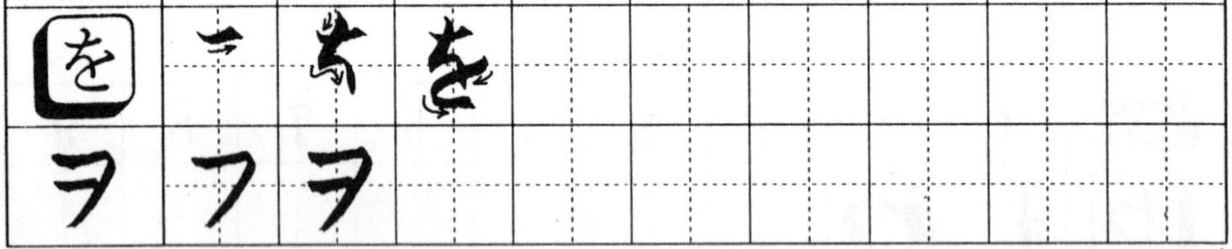

ONE STROKE

Today's Target Kana For Stroke Practice

Last Kana	Hiragana Soft Cursive Writing	Katakana Stiff Square Strokes	Next Kana
を	ん	ン	が
O			GA

Hints For Stroke Order Reproduction And Recognition

(ん-**un**), which sounds like the 'n' in "gin", is the pronunciation of this kana. For the best stroke writing results, use a felt tip pen. Start from the left and follow the arrows. Using the very first kana as an example, slowly, with a light steady hand, try to accurately form your target kana. Use all the blank box spaces and imitate the strokes of your present and last kana until your kana resemble the original ones.

Target Strokes	1	2	3	4	5	6	7	8	9
ん	ん								
ン	ヽ	ン							

Basic Kana (わ-Wa) To (ん-Un) Stroke Order

CREATIVE KANA REVIEW

Write it! Read it! Say it!

わ		を		ん
WA		O		UN

LINK-A-LETTER: You have already practiced writing all the hiragana on this page. Now use them to build new words in the adjoining boxes. Then try to link them to phrases.

わけ **wake** reason				わら **wara** straw			
うん **un** yes, I see				うんちん **unchin** fares			
わかる **wakaru** understand				うんゆ **unyu** transport			
わかれ **wakare** to part				うんてん **unten** to drive			
えん **en** yen(currency)				えをみる **e o miru** look at a picture			

SEARCH AND MATCH IDENTICAL KANA 121

Expand your kana recognition ability. Search within the numbers (1-5) for the kana which matches the left hand column Romanized letters. Write the correct kana in the blank boxes. Then use the bottom page boxes to practice any kana you wish.

EXAMPLE:

			1	2	3	4	5
			↓	↓	↓	↓	↓
ga	←	3	だ	な	が	み	ぱ

Mark your correct answer numbers in these boxes below			1	2	3	4	5
		⬇	⬇	⬇	⬇	⬇	⬇
da	⬅		る	だ	ぱ	ん	い
mi	⬅		や	ゆ	み	け	ら
chi	⬅		き	じ	ん	さ	ち
wa	⬅		ま	れ	わ	め	ね
he	⬅		つ	ん	へ	う	ひ

Practice writing any kana in these boxes

122 Vocabulary Expanding For Interacting
Receiving And Giving Advice Convincingly

NATURAL SURVIVAL CONVERSATION

What You Might Hear	How You Might Possibly Answer
(O) **Kare no chikara o kaikaburi sugimashita.** (E) It looks like we really over-estimated him.	(C) **Jibun de shite miru ga ii.** (M) It would be better for you to try doing it by yourself.
(O) **Sō yū koto wa shinai hō ga iin desu.** (E) It would be best not to do such a thing.	(O) **Jijō ni yorimasu.** (E) It all depends.
(O) **Seiji-san wa seijitsu dewa nai.** (E) Mr. Seiji is insincere.	(P) **Mattaku hantai desu. Watashi wa kare o yoku shitte iru no de.** (E) I totally disagree with you because I know him well.
(C) **Kare ni yarashi toke** (*or*) **Hottoke!** (M) Don't persuade him from doing that.	(P) **Wakarimashita. Watashi no shitsumon ni kotaete kudasatte arigatō.** (E) Oh, I see. Thanks for answering my question.
(O) **Ichido ni futatsu no koto ga dekiru.** (E) I can do two things at once.	(C) **Jōtatsu suru koto wa ii koto da!** (M) It's good to improve on what you're doing.
(P) **Kono ten de genkai desu.** (E) I've reached my limit at this point.	(P) **Watashi no mikata kara minai no desu ka?** (E) Why don't you look at it from my point of view?
(P) **Go-jogen o kudasaimasen ka?** (E) Would you mind giving me some advice?	(P) **Ningen kankei ni motto kyōmi o shimesu yō ni chūkoku shimasu.** (E) I'd advise you to take more interest in human relations.
(C) **Hatsu mimi desu!** (E) That's the first time I've heard that.	(P) **Donna mono nimo hajimete to yū koto ga arimasu.** (E) There's a first time for everything.
(P) **Umaku ikuka dō ka shirimasen.** (E) I don't know whether it'll come or not.	(P) **Yasashii ketsudan dewa arimasen.** (E) It's not an easy decision to make.

NATURAL SURVIVAL CONVERSATION

What You Might Hear	How You Might Possibly Answer
(O) **Piitā o hōmon suru yō Jodi wa teian shimashita.** (E) Jodi suggested that I call on Peter.	(C) **Ikanai hō ga ii.** (E) It would be best not to go.
(O) **Mizu o karada kara fukitoritai.** (E) I want to dry myself off.	(P) **Kono taoru de karada o fuite kudasai.** (E) Please wipe yourself down with this towel.
(P) **Doa o shikkari shimete kudasai.** (E) Shut the door tightly.	(O) **Wakatta. Suru wa yo.** (W) I understand. I'll do that.

Receiving And Giving Advice Convincingly

19) Shoji wa soji suru tame ni shoji o aketa.
Mr. Shoji opened the sliding doors to clean up. (original)

20) Sumomo mo momo mo momo no uchi.
Sumomo and peach are the same kind of a peach.

21) Tonari no kyaku wa yoku kaki kuu kyaku da ! Uchi no kyaku wa kaki kuwan kyaku, kaki kuu kyaku to kaki kuwan kyaku.
The guest near door eats persimmons. Our guest does not eat persimmons. A guest who eats persimmons and a guest who does not eat persimmons.

124 Nigori (") And Handaku (°) Marked Sounds Basic Kana (が-Ga) To (ご-Go) Stroke Order

Ganbare yo!
Do your best!

Gakidomo ga kaette kita.
The kiddies came home.

Kore de watashi mo kata no ni ga orosesō desu yo.
What a load off my shoulders!

Guzu-guzu suru na!
Don't be slow!

Kare ni gūzen atta.
I bumped into him.

Genki ga deru.
Is revived.

Genkan de matsu.
Wait in the entrance.

Gizensha da!
He's a hypocrit.

Ginkō ni iku.
I'm going to the bank.

Ano densha ni giri-giri mani-ai-mashita.
I was just able to catch the train.

Gomen nasai.
I'm sorry.

Gokai shinai de.
Don't misunderstand me.

FIVE STROKES

Today's Target Kana For Stroke Practice

Last Kana	Hiragana Soft Cursive Writing	Katakana Stiff Square Strokes	Next Kana
ん	が	ガ	ぎ
UN			GI

Hints For Stroke Order Reproduction And Recognition

(が-**ga**), like the 'ga' beginning words such as "garden" or "garlic," is usually pronounced very hard. But when it appears in the middle of a word it is softly nasalized like the 'ng' of "king" or "song." 'Ga' when used as a particle still gets the same pronunciation. Two short bars (゛) and a circle(゜) placed to the upper right of a consonant indicates that it should be voiced with close to vibrating vocal chords.

Target Strokes	1	2	3	4	5	6	7	8	9
が	う	カ	か	が	が				
ガ	フ	カ	か	ガ					

SIX STROKES

Today's Target Kana For Stroke Practice

Last Kana	Hiragana Soft Cursive Writing	Katakana Stiff Square Strokes	Next Kana
が	ぎ	ギ	ぐ
GA			GU

Hints For Stroke Order Reproduction And Recognition

(ぎ-**gi**), which sounds like the English word "gee", is the pronunciation of this kana. For the best stroke writing results, use a felt tip pen. Start from the left and follow the arrows. Using the very first kana as an example, slowly, with a light steady hand, try to accurately form your target kana. Use all the blank box spaces and imitate the strokes of your present and last kana until your kana resemble the original ones.

Target Strokes	1	2	3	4	5	6	7	8	9
ぎ						ぎ			
ギ	一	二	キ	ギ	ギ				

THREE STROKES

Today's Target Kana For Stroke Practice

Last Kana	Hiragana	Katakana	Next Kana
ぎ	ぐ	グ	げ
GI	Hiragana Soft Cursive Writing	Katakana Stiff Square Strokes	GE

Hints For Stroke Order Reproduction And Recognition

(ぐ-**gu**), which sounds like the beginning of "goose", is the pronunciation of this kana. For the best stroke writing results, use a felt tip pen. Start from the left and follow the arrows. Using the very first kana as an example, slowly, with a light steady hand, try to accurately form your target kana. Use all the blank box spaces and imitate the strokes of your present and last kana until your kana resemble the original ones.

Target Strokes	1	2	3	4	5	6	7	8	9
ぐ	く	ぐ	ぐ						
グ	ノ	ク	グ	グ					

Basic Kana (が-Ga) To (ご-Go) Stroke Order

FIVE STROKES

Today's Target Kana For Stroke Practice

Last Kana	Hiragana Soft Cursive Writing	Katakana Stiff Square Strokes	Next Kana
ぐ	げ	ゲ	ご
GU			GO

Hints For Stroke Order Reproduction And Recognition

(げ-**ge**), which sounds like the beginning of the English word "guess", is the pronunciation of this kana. For the best stroke writing results, use a felt tip pen. Start from the left and follow the arrows. Using the very first kana as an example, slowly, with a light steady hand, try to accurately form your target kana. Use all the blank box spaces and imitate the strokes of your present and last kana until your kana resemble the original ones.

Target Strokes	1	2	3	4	5	6	7	8	9
げ	|	に	げ	げ	げ				
ゲ	ノ	ト	ケ	ゲ	ゲ				

FOUR STROKES

Today's Target Kana For Stroke Practice

Last Kana			Next Kana
げ	ご	ゴ	ざ
GE	Hiragana Soft Cursive Writing	Katakana Stiff Square Strokes	ZA

Hints For Stroke Order Reproduction And Recognition

(ご-**go**), which sounds exactly like the English word "go", is the pronunciation of this kana. For the best stroke writing results, use a felt tip pen. Start from the left and follow the arrows. Using the very first kana as an example, slowly, with a light steady hand, try to accurately form your target kana. Use all the blank box spaces and imitate the strokes of your present and last kana until your kana resemble the original ones.

Target Strokes	1	2	3	4	5	6	7	8	9
ご									
ゴ	フ	コ	ゴ	ゴ					

Basic Kana (が-Ga) To (ご-Go) Stroke Order

CREATIVE KANA REVIEW
Write it! Read it! Say it!

が	ぎ	ぐ	げ	ご
GA	GI	GU	GE	GO

LINK-A-LETTER: You have already practiced writing all the hiragana on this page. Now use them to build new words in the adjoining boxes. Then try to link them to phrases.

がき **gaki** brat				ごみ **gomi** trash			
ぎり **giri** obligation				げんき **genki** healthy			
ぐち **guchi** complaint				ごま **goma** sesame			
げり **geri** loose bowels				ぎんこう **ginkō** bank			
ぐらい **gurai** about				ごい **goi** vocabulary			

Governing Particles (kakari-joshi) 131

Particles in this category can be combined with various parts of speech, governing what precedes them to give a specialized meaning.

か

In Japanese grammar, a cue to indicate an interrogative sentence is the question particle '**ka**' found at the end of a sentence. But you must always be sure to get the question intonation correct. This particle, in conjunction with question words, also indicates that event or time denoted by the interrogatives is uncertain. When it is combined with concrete nouns it expresses a choice between the matters involved.

Example :
Nani ka goyō desu ka ?
Do you have any business to conduct with me ?

は

This is the hiragana for the particle '**wa**' . Being an emphatic nominative, this topic marker is chiefly used when the subject is to be emphasized. Its original pronunciation is '**ha**' but is pronounced as '**wa**' when used as a particle.

こそ

The particle "**koso**" serves as an intensifier and can be combined with any part of speech for emphasizing purposes.

Example :
Watashi koso ayamarimasu.
It is I who ought to apologize.

さえ

The particle "**sae**" emphasizes the precise identity of the matter or matters which it governs.

Example :
Ano hito wa namae sae kakenai.
That person can't even write his own name.

132 ## Governing Particles (kakari-joshi)

でも

The particle "**demo**" governs a word or words to imply modesty or to give a vague assertion rather than a negative one.

Example :

Ocha <u>demo</u> nomi mashō.

Let's have some tea or some such thing.

DOODLE Fun With Hiragana Combinations

Every line drawn in each doodle facial expression represents a hiragana ideogram. When read and spoken they sound comical. Try your hand in the art of hiragana doodling, which goes back to the Edo Period or earlier. It's an excellent instant method for pronouncing, writing, reading and remembering hiragana. Surprise your Japanese acquaintances with your ability to imitate and duplicate their mother tongue in such an amusing way.

へのへのもへじ

Honest farmer called Moheji.

へのへのくつも

Treat your shoes kindly.

へのへのもへの

Be careful of your goods.

つる三八〇〇ムし

Tsuru City is terrible.

いののうやう

Good view of Noh stage pine.

へのへのしこし

Go go shikoku.

See Page 122

SEARCH FOR THE CORRECT SENTENCES THESE WORDS COME FROM. THEN, WITH THE INCLUSION OF THESE WORDS, PRACTICE WRITING THE COMPLETE SENTENCE IN HIRAGANA. THEN READ THEM ALOUD FOR ACCURATE PRONUNCIATION AND PROPER PACING.

134 Vocabulary Expanding For Interacting

Adverbs of Time

NATURAL SURVIVAL CONVERSATION

What You Might Hear	How You Might Possibly Answer
(C) **Mata ashita no kaigi no iro-iro na koto o wasureta.** (E) Again, I've forgotten many facts about tomorrow's meeting.	(P) **Maiban watashi wa tsugi no hi no keikaku o kimemasu.** (E) I plan the next day's schedule every night.
(P) **Watashi-tachi wa biyōin ni mada ikimasu ka ?** (W) Are we still going to the beauty salon ?	(P) **Mamonaku raikyaku ga aru yotei desu.** (E) I'm expecting a visitor very shortly.
(P) **Itsumo nanika sagashite imasu.** (E) I'm always searching for something.	(P) **Ato de hanashimashō.** (E) Let's talk about that later.
(C) **Watashi niwa ame ga romantikku ni kanji nai.** (E) I don't feel that rain is romantic.	(P) **Shikashi ame wa nōgyō niwa taisetsu desu.** (E) But rain is valuable to farmers.
(O) **Jikan ga totte mo hayaku sugita.** (E) The time passed very quickly.	(O) **Anata kara mae ni kikimashita.** (E) I've heard that from you before.
(C) **Kondo no renshū wa itsu ni shiyō ?** (E) When shall we practice next ?	(P) **Kono saigo no keikaku ga shōnin sareta ato desu.** (E) After this final plan is approved.
(C) **Hai, mamonaku suru to seigaku no gakushū shinakereba.** (E) Yes and shortly after that I must take voice lessons.	(P) **Chotto jikan o itadakitai no desu ga.** (E) Do you have a few free moments ?
(O) **"Watashi wa totsuzen ima sugu dōshite mo dekakenakereba naranai." to kare wa itta.** (E) Suddenly he said "I must leave at once".	(P) **Shikashi ima koko ni kita bakari desu.** (E) But I've just arrived.
(P) **Dōzo shibaraku matte kudasai.** (E) Please wait a moment.	(O) **Mō mamonaku ginkō wa shimarimasu.** (E) The bank will close any time now.

NATURAL SURVIVAL CONVERSATION

What You Might Hear	How You Might Possibly Answer
(P) **Gūzen yakusoku o omoidashimashita.** (E) I remembered my appointment by chance.	(P) **Itte kimasu.** (*or*) **Itte mairimasu.** (E) I'm going now. (but will return later)
(P) **Mata dōzo.** (*or*) **Mata irasshai.** (E) Please come again.	(P) **Arigatō gozaimasu.** (E) Thank you very much.

Twist Your Tongue With These Tongue Twisters

22) Tokyo Tokkyo-kyoka kyoku kyoku-chō.
Head of the Department of Patent Approval.

23) Tsuki zukini tsuki miru tsuki wa ōkeredo tsuki miru tsuki wa kono tsuki no tsuki.
Every month we see the moon every day, every night, but tonight's moon is different from other moons.

24) Ura niwa ni wa niwa, niwa ni wa niwa, niwatori ga iru.
There are two chickens in the backyard garden and two chickens in the garden.

136

Nigori (゛) And Handaku (゜) Marked Sounds
Basic Kana (ざ-za) to (ぞ-zo) Stroke Order

Zannen desu.
It's too bad.

Zasshi o yomu.
Read a magazine.

Zainichi gaikokujin ni yasashiku shiro.
Be nicer to foreigners in Japan.

Jinsei wa tanoshii.
My life is happy.

Jiro-jiro miru na!
Don't gape at me!

Jikan ga nai.
I have no time.

Jishin wa kowai.
I'm afraid of earthquakes.

Zutto matsu.
I waited a long time.

Zurui yarikata da.
It's a cunning way.

Zuibun nagai denwa da.
It's a real long telephone call.

Zenbu urikirechū.
It's all sold out.

Zeitaku o suru.
Is extravagant.

Zōkin de sōji suru.
Wipe with a cloth.

Kare wa zotto suru.
He's scared.

FIVE STROKES

Today's Target Kana For Stroke Practice

Last Kana	Hiragana Soft Cursive Writing	Katakana Stiff Square Strokes	Next Kana
ご	ざ	ザ	じ
GO			JI

Hints For Stroke Order Reproduction And Recognition

(**ざ-za**), which is the pronunciation of this kana, is similar to the first sound of the male name "Zachary." For the best stroke writing results, use a felt tip pen. Start from the left and follow the arrows. Using the very first kana as an example, slowly, with a light steady hand, try to accurately form your target kana. Use all the blank box spaces and imitate the strokes of your present and last kana until your kana resemble the original ones.

Target Strokes	1	2	3	4	5	6	7	8	9
ざ									
ザ									

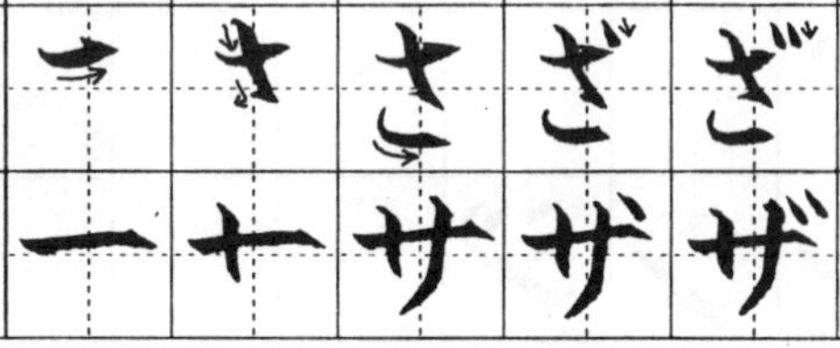

Basic Kana (ざ-Za) To (ぞ-Zo) Stroke Order

THREE STROKES

Today's Target Kana For Stroke Practice

Last Kana	Hiragana Soft Cursive Writing	Katakana Stiff Square Strokes	Next Kana
ざ	じ	ジ	ず
ZA			ZU

Hints For Stroke Order Reproduction And Recognition

(じ-**ji**) or (**zi**), which is the pronunciation of this kana, is similar to the first sound of the word "zipper." For the best stroke writing results, use a felt tip pen. Start from the left and follow the arrows. Using the very first kana as an example, slowly, with a light steady hand, try to accurately form your target kana. Use all the blank box spaces and imitate the strokes of your present and last kana until your kana resemble the original ones.

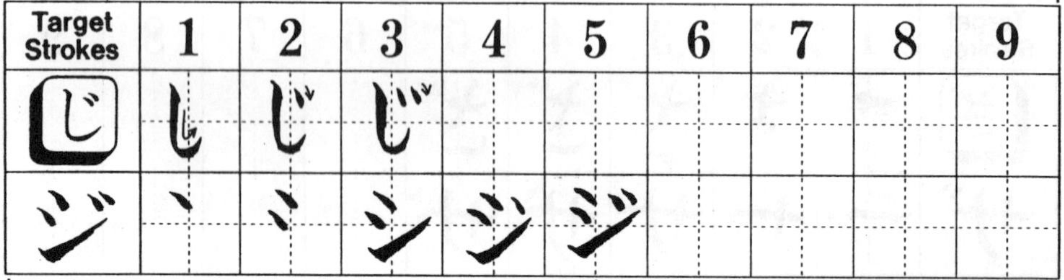

FOUR STROKES

Today's Target Kana For Stroke Practice

Last Kana	Hiragana Soft Cursive Writing	Katakana Stiff Square Strokes	Next Kana
じ	ず	ズ	ぜ
JI			ZE

Hints For Stroke Order Reproduction And Recognition

(**ず-zu**), which is the pronunciation of this kana, is similar to the first sound of the word "zoo." For the best stroke writing results, use a felt tip pen. Start from the left and follow the arrows. Using the very first kana as an example, slowly, with a light steady hand, try to accurately form your target kana. Use all the blank box spaces and imitate the strokes of your present and last kana until your kana resemble the original ones.

Target Strokes	1	2	3	4	5	6	7	8	9
ず	一	す	ず	ず					
ズ	フ	ス	ズ	ズ					

Basic Kana (ざ-Za) To (ぞ-Zo) Stroke Order

FIVE STROKES

Today's Target Kana For Stroke Practice

Last Kana	Hiragana	Katakana	Next Kana
ず	ぜ	ゼ	ぞ
ZU	Hiragana Soft Cursive Writing	Katakana Stiff Square Strokes	ZO

Hints For Stroke Order Reproduction And Recognition

(ぜ-ze), which is the pronunciation of this kana, is similar to the first sound of the female name "Zena." For the best stroke writing results, use a felt tip pen. Start from the left and follow the arrows. Using the very first kana as an example, slowly, with a light steady hand, try to accurately form your target kana. Use all the blank box spaces and imitate the strokes of your present and last kana until your kana resemble the original ones.

Target Strokes	1	2	3	4	5	6	7	8	9

FOUR STROKES

Today's Target Kana For Stroke Practice

Last Kana			Next Kana
ぜ	ぞ	ゾ	だ
ZE	Hiragana Soft Cursive Writing	Katakana Stiff Square Strokes	DA

Hints For Stroke Order Reproduction And Recognition

(**ぞ-zo**), which is the pronunciation of this kana, is similar to the first sound in the word "zone." For the best stroke writing results, use a felt tip pen. Start from the left and follow the arrows. Using the very first kana as an example, slowly, with a light steady hand, try to accurately form your target kana. Use all the blank box spaces and imitate the strokes of your present and last kana until your kana resemble the original ones.

Target Strokes	1	2	3	4	5	6	7	8	9
ぞ				ぞ					
ゾ	丶	ソ	ゾ	ゾ					

Basic Kana (ざ-Zo) To (ぞ-Zo) Stroke Order

CREATIVE KANA REVIEW

Write it! Read it! Say it!

ざ	じ	ず	ぜ	ぞ
ZA	ji(ZI)	ZU	ZE	ZO

LINK-A-LETTER: You have already practiced writing all the hiragana on this page. Now use them to build new words in the adjoining boxes. Then try to link them to phrases.

ざんきん **zankin** balance	ちず **chizu** map
ずいひつ **zuihitsu** essay	ざっし **zasshi** magazine
ぜんぜん **zenzen** nothing	ぜひ **zehi** by all means
じ **ji** alphabetical letter	ぞう **zō** an elephant
ぞく **zoku** group, tribe	じんこう **jinkō** people

SEARCH AND MATCH IDENTICAL KANA

Expand your kana recognition ability. Search within the numbers (1-5) for the kana which matches the left hand column Romanized letters. Write the correct kana in the blank boxes. Then use the bottom page boxes to practice any kana you wish.

EXAMPLE:

Answer

			1	2	3	4	5
			↓	↓	↓	↓	↓
ga	←	3	だ	な	が	み	ぱ

Mark your correct answer numbers in these boxes below			1	2	3	4	5
		⬇	⬇	⬇	⬇	⬇	⬇
shi	⬅		せ	し	そ	さ	す
na	⬅		の	に	ね	ぬ	な
o	⬅		あ	こ	を	ち	りゃ
u	⬅		ら	よ	や	う	で
ni	⬅		い	こ	り	に	え

Practice writing any kana in these boxes

144 Vocabulary Expanding For Interacting

Continuation Of Giving Advice

NATURAL SURVIVAL CONVERSATION

What You Might Hear	How You Might Possibly Answer
(P) **Kyū ni itami o kanji-mashita.** (E) I felt a sudden pain.	(O) **Watashi no chūkoku o kiite sugu ni isha ni mite morainasai.** (M) Take my advice. Go to see a doctor at once.
(O) **Kurisu wa beddo no ue de utsubuse ni natte yasunde iru.** (E) Chris is laying on the bed resting.	(O) **Kare no jama o suru to ikenai.** (E) Then you mustn't disturb him.
(P) **Tabemono ga tanegire ni natta yō desu. Waratte wa ikemasen.** (E) We seem to be all out of food. You mustn't laugh.	(O) **Hayaku soto e itte mō sukoshi kainasai.** (E) Why don't you quickly go out and buy some.
(O) **Sono kaisha ni nitsū-me no tegami o okurimasu.** (E) I will send that company a second letter.	(P) **Moshi watashi dattara mō tegami wa okuri masen** (E) If I were you I would not send any more.
(O) **Ware-ware wa gokagetsukan awanakatta.** (E) We did not meet for five months.	(O) **Kaigi wa ni-nen ni ichi-do hiraka-remasu.** (E) A meeting was held bi-annually.
(C) **Japano-san niwa komatta mono desu ne.** (E) Mr. Japano is certainly annoying.	(O) **Sō desu ne. Itsumo kōdō ga hitori-yogari nan desu.** (E) I'll say. He always acts as though his opinion is the only one that counts.
(O) **Kuchi-biru no ugoki o yomima-shita.** (E) I read your lips.	(P) **Watashi o shinyō shinasai. Karera wa mattaku wakatte inai no desu.** (E) Take it from me, they just don't understand.
(P) **Konban otomari ni narimasu ka?** (E) Would you like to stay overnight?	(O) **Go-meiwaku janakereba toma-rimasu.** (E) Yes, if it's no trouble I don't mind.
(O) **Kore de ii desu.** (E) This will do.	(P) **Sukoshi hayaku kaette mo ii desu ka?** (E) Is it alright if I leave a little early?

Vocabulary Expanding For Interacting

Continuation Of Giving Advice

NATURAL SURVIVAL CONVERSATION

What You Might Hear	How You Might Possibly Answer
(O) **Tabako no shirushi wa nan desu ka?** (E) What symbolizes a cigarette?	(O) **Ippō no hashi ni hi soshite tahō no hashi ni oroka mono.** (E) A fire on one end and a fool on the other.
(O) **Mikka-kan tsuzukete kinasai to isha ga itta.** (E) The doctor said, I must come three days straight.	(O) **Kuchi o fusaide kudasai. Anata no baikin nanka hoshiku arimasen.** (E) Please cover your mouth. I don't want your germs.
(O) **Shufutachi wa henna onna ga kono hen ni sunde iru to iimasu.** (E) The housewives say a weird woman lives in this area.	(O) **Rinjin kara itsumo uwasa o kiite imasu.** (E) I always hear rumors from the neighbors.
(O) **Ii hōseki o erabu no ga jōzu desu ne.** (E) You have good taste in jewellery selection.	(O) **O seji o itte imasu ne.** (W) You are flattering me.

Twist Your Tongue With These Tongue Twisters

25) **Uri uri ga uri uri ni kite uri uri nokoshi uri uri kaeru uri uri no koe.**
A melon seller comes to sell melons but he didn't sell all the melons. He was selling the melons to go back home.

26) **Yamanashi ni nashi wa nashi rashii!**
It seems there are no pears in Yamanashi (Prefecture). (original)

146 Nigori (゛) And Handaku (゜) Marked Sounds Basic Kana (だ-Da) To (ど-Do) Stroke Order

Daijōbu.
It's okay.

Damari nasai.
Shut up!

Mikake daoshi desu ne.
Looks can be deceiving.

Hanaji ga deru.
I'm bleeding.

Kubi o chijimeta.
He only shrugged his shoulders.

Denki o tsukeru.
Turn on the light.

Mō denakucha.
I have to go.

Denwa o kakenaku-cha.
I have to make a phone call.

Kare wa kodomo zure de kita.
He came with his child.

Mudazukai ga ōi.
He wastes a lot of money.

Dōzo kochira e.
This way, please.

Dōmo arigatō.
Thank you very much.

Doke!
Get out of the way!

SIX STROKES

Today's Target Kana For Stroke Practice

Last Kana	Hiragana Soft Cursive Writing	Katakana Stiff Square Strokes	Next Kana
ぞ	だ	ダ	ぢ
ZO			JI

Hints For Stroke Order Reproduction And Recognition

(だ-**da**) is the pronunciation of this kana, which is similar to the first sound of the city "Dakar." For the best stroke writing results, use a felt tip pen. Start from the left and follow the arrows. Using the very first kana as an example, slowly, with a light steady hand, try to accurately form your target kana. Use all the blank box spaces and imitate the strokes of your present and last kana until your kana resemble the original ones.

Target Strokes	1	2	3	4	5	6	7	8	9
だ					だ	だ			
ダ	ノ	ク	タ	ダ	ダ				

Basic Kana (だ-Da) To (ど-Do) Stroke Order

FOUR	Today's Target Kana For Stroke Practice		STROKES
Last Kana	ぢ	ヂ	Next Kana
だ	Hiragana Soft Cursive Writing	Katakana Stiff Square Strokes	づ
DA			ZU

Hints For Stroke Order Reproduction And Recognition

(**ぢ-ji**) (or) (**zi**) is the pronunciation of this kana, which is similar to the first sound of the word "jeep." As explained earlier in this book, there is no distinction between the sounds of the syllables (ぢ) and (じ), and between (づ) and (ず).

Target Strokes	1	2	3	4	5	6	7	8	9
ぢ	一	ち	ぢ	ぢ					
ヂ	ノ	二	チ	ヂ	ヂ				

THREE STROKES

Today's Target Kana For Stroke Practice

Last Kana	Hiragana Soft Cursive Writing	Katakana Stiff Square Strokes	Next Kana
ぢ	づ	ヅ	で
JI			DE

Hints For Stroke Order Reproduction And Recognition

(**づ-zu**), the pronunciation of this kana, is rather similar to the first sound of "Zulu," the name of an East African tribe. For the best stroke writing results, use a felt tip pen. Start from the left and follow the arrows. Using the very first kana as an example, slowly, with a light steady hand, try to accurately form your target kana. Use all the blank box spaces and imitate the strokes of your present and last kana until your kana resemble the original ones.

Target Strokes	1	2	3	4	5	6	7	8	9
づ	つ	づ	づ						
ヅ	丶	丶丶	ツ	ヅ	ヅ				

THREE	Today's Target Kana For Stroke Practice		STROKES
Last Kana	で	デ	Next Kana
づ	Hiragana Soft Cursive Writing	Katakana Stiff Square Strokes	ど
ZU			DO

Hints For Stroke Order Reproduction And Recognition

(で-**de**), the pronunciation of this kana, is similar to the first sound in the female name "Denise." For the best stroke writing results, use a felt tip pen. Start from the left and follow the arrows. Using the very first kana as an example, slowly, with a light steady hand, try to accurately form your target kana. Use all the blank box spaces and imitate the strokes of your present and last kana until your kana resemble the original ones.

Target Strokes	1	2	3	4	5	6	7	8	9
で	て	で	で						
デ	ー	ニ	テ	デ	デ				

FOUR STROKES

Today's Target Kana For Stroke Practice

Last Kana	Hiragana Soft Cursive Writing	Katakana Stiff Square Strokes	Next Kana
で	ど	ド	ば
DE			BA

Hints For Stroke Order Reproduction And Recognition

(**ど-do**), which is the pronunciation of this kana, is similar to the first sound of "dough" for making bread. For the best stroke writing results use a felt tip pen. Start from the left and follow the arrows. Using the first kana as an example, slowly, with a light steady hand, try to accurately form your very first kana. Use all the blank box spaces and repeat until your kana resemble the original ones.

Target Strokes	1	2	3	4	5	6	7	8	9
ど	｜	と	ど	ど					
ド	｜	ト	ド	ド					

Basic Kana (だ-Da) To (ど-Do) Stroke Order

CREATIVE KANA REVIEW

Write it! Read it! Say it!

だ	ぢ	づ	で	ど
DA	JI	ZU	DE	DO

LINK-A-LETTER: You have already practiced writing all the hiragana on this page. Now use them to build new words in the adjoining boxes. Then try to link them to phrases.

どうせ **dōse** after all				どうもどうも **dōmo dōmo** thank you			
であう **deau** meet				どうそうせい **dōsōsei** class mate			
できる **dekiru** can do				でんきゅう **denkyū** light bulb			
だけ **dake** only				つづり **tuzuri** spelling			
どうぞ **dōzo** please				ちぢれげ **chijirege** curly hair			

Examples Of How Auxiliary Particles Are Used 153

Auxiliary Particles **(Joshi)**

Appearing in separate categories throughout the book, these Japanese grammatical particles are placed after the words they govern. Observe them carefully, as they are the keys to correct Japanese grammar.

Casual Particles (**Kaku-joshi**)

Particles appearing in this group are used chiefly in providing nouns and pronouns casual relationships.

が

(が-**ga**) This nominative case auxiliary particle is an object marker as well as subject marker.

Example sentences:

(nominative) **Demotai ga yatte kimashita.**
A Strike is taking place.

Shizukada ga sukoshi sabishii.
It's quiet but a little lonely.
(but . . . conjunction)

で

(で-**de**) which indicates 'at', 'for' or 'manner of' is used to relate to the means, cause, way, and place of an action. You'd express prepositions by attaching **de**, **ni**, and **e**, after nouns.

Example sentences:

Anata wa doko de sore o kaimashita ka?
At what place did you buy that?

Kinō Isetan de.
Yesterday at Isetan Department Store.

(standard) for (in) **Nihon de ichiban takai tokoro wa doko desu ka?**
What area in Japan is the most expensive?

(by) **Shigoto wa denwa de sumasemashita.**
I finished my work by phone.

154 Examples Of How Auxiliary Particles Are Used

(caused by) **Kare wa kaji de shinimashita.**
He died in a fire.

(like a conjunction)
Kimi wa benkyō shinai de asonde bakari iru.
You don't study but rather play a lot.

に

(に-**ni**) which relates to 'in', 'place' or 'point of time' indicates the termination of verbal acts, what is suffered, acted upon, locality, time, etc.

Example sentences :

(at) or (in) **Anata wa Shinjuku ni sunde iru no desu ne !**
You live in Shinjuku don't you ?

(from) **Kare ni kiite kudasai.**
Please hear it from him.

(purpose) **Kare wa Ginza e kaimono ni ikimashita.**
He went to Ginza to do some shopping.

(accusative) **Kinō kyūyū ni aimashita.**
Yesterday I met an old friend.

(exception) Asa to ban ni kare wa shimbun o haitatsushimasu.
He delivers newspapers from morning till evening.

(to) **Kinō Yotsuya ni itta.**
Yesterday I went to Yotsuya district.

の

(の-**no**) is used as an object marker in a possessive case, plus it supplies the appositive relationship.

Examples Of How Auxiliary Particles Are Used 155

を

(を-**o**) is used in the accusative case, and expresses the object to which the action of transitive verbs is directed. In case of intransitives, it indicates the locality in which the verbal action takes place.

Example sentences :

Watashi wa kare o yoku shitte imasu.
I know him very well.

Dōzo okashi o meshi agatte kudasai.
Please have some sweets.

Sono biru no kado o magaru to sugu desu.
It's located shortly after turning the corner of that building.

へ

(へ-**e**) This casual particle indicates the direction, locality, receiver of the act of either giving or sending, etc.

Example sentences :

(to) **Benito-san wa doko e ikimashita ka?**
Where did Mr. Benito go?

Kare wa jimusho e ikimashita.
He went to the office.

から

(から-**kara**) which indicates 'from', also indicates the starting point of a verbal action.

Example sentence :

Dare kara ano uwasa o kikimashita ka?
From whom did you hear that rumor?

156 Examples Of How Auxiliary Particles Are Used

や

(や-**ya**) is a variant of the nominative particle. It is used when two or more different kinds of things are juxtaposed.

Example sentence :

Ichigo ya momo ya budō ga hitsuyō desu.
Strawberries, peaches and grapes are necessary.

お

ご

The prefix (お-**o**) or (ご-**go**) makes a word honorific when placed before a noun to infer a thing is in the possession of the person you're speaking to. Using either prefix is a sign of respect.

Example sentences :

(P) **O namae wa nan desu ka?**
(E) What is your name?

(P) **Go-kazoku wa inai desu ka?**
(E) Are your parents in?

* Never add the honorific word '**san**' to your name when referring to yourself in Japanese. It should only be used to refer to other persons.

Example : Michael-san (or) Takagi-san

You'd express an objective case by attaching **o** (sometimes refered to as **wo**), after a noun.

Example :

(O) **Kōen de kōen-san wa tada no kōen o okonatta.**
(E) Mr. Koen gave a free lecture in the park.

Kōen (suru)	**Kōen**	**Kōen**
Performance	Park	Lecture

(Point Out What's Wrong)

Remembering what you have already read regarding stroke order, carefully note how these strokes are written. See how you measure up.

This → ぢ is the correct stroke in stead of this → ぢ

Notice how the correct stroke begins and ends. Now check and see what you may have done wrong. Check one (1) box with an 'X'.

This stroke because じ is wrong it was written

Above the line	Below the line	It's okay
☐	☐	☐

This stroke because せ is wrong it was drawn

Too short	Too long	It's okay
☐	☐	☐

The correct stroke line goes upwards ね

To the right	To the left	It's okay
☐	☐	☐

Put a check mark below each wrongly stroked kana and write the correct way it should appear in the spare boxes and pronounce each kana aloud with your Japanese 'kana helpmate'.

Review strokes →	や	な	ふ	ほ
Your stroke →				

158 WORD AND SENTENCE SEARCHING FOR WRITING PRACTICE

See Page 144

SEARCH FOR THE CORRECT SENTENCE THESE WORDS COME FROM. THEN, WITH THE INCLUSION OF THESE WORDS, PRACTICE WRITING THE COMPLETE SENTENCE IN HIRAGANA. THEN READ THEM ALOUD FOR ACCURATE PRONUNCIATION AND PROPER PACING.

NATURAL SURVIVAL CONVERSATION

What You Might Hear	How You Might Possibly Answer
(C) **Wakaru ka na?** (M) I wonder if you understand me?	(C) **Anata wa baka to hanashite iru no ja nai.** (E) You're not speaking to a dummy.
(C) **Wakaranai darō na?** (M) I assume you don't understand.	(P) **Mittsu no daigaku de benkyō shimashita. Anata wa?** (E) I attended three universities. And you?
(C) **Kare wa nikumenai na!** (M) You can't hate him even if you try.	(O) **Saikin kare o mikakenai no de watashi wa kankei nai.** (E) I haven't seen him lately so I'm not getting involved.
(O) **O de mukae ni ikun desu ne?** (E) You're going to meet up with him, aren't you?	(C) **Sō da yo!** (E) That's right!
(C) **Ano ne doko ka itte kurenai ka?** (E) Excuse me can you go some place for me?	(C) **Iku zo?** (E) I'm gonna go!
(O) **Kimi wa mō konain da ne.** (M) You're not coming anymore, are you?	(O) **Kikai ga areba mata kimasu.** (E) I will come again if I have a chance.
(C) **Yappari kimi wa yasashii hito da.** (M) You're as kind as I had expected.	(P) **Sukoshi demo oyaku ni tateba ureshii desu.** (E) I shall be happy to be of any help I can.
(O) **Jissai ni wa gyaku nan desu.** (E) Actually, it's the opposite.	(C) **Wakaru tomo.** (E) Of course I can understand it.
(C) **Kare wa hondana o sute-chau. Anata wa iru no?** (E) He's throwing away his bookcase. Do you need it?	(C) **Kurerun dattara morau tomo.** (M) If he gives it to me of course I'll take it.

160 Vocabulary Expanding For Interacting

Usage Of Final Particles

NATURAL SURVIVAL CONVERSATION

What You Might Hear	How You Might Possibly Answer
(O) **Kyō wa kinyōbi na no ni nichiyōbi no yō da.** (E) Although it's Friday it seems like Sunday.	(O) **Me ga takai.** (E) You're a good judge of things.
(O) **Watashi wa anata dake o tayori ni shite iru.** (E) I depend only on you.	(C) **Ore dake o tayoru na.** (E) Don't depend only on me.
(C) **Hitori-yogari datta ka na.** (E) Was I doing things a bit too much on my own, perhaps ?	(O) **Yamuo e nai.** (E) It couldn't be helped.
(O) **Makase nasai.** (E) Please leave everything to me.	(O) **Sore wa ii kangae no yō da ne.** (M) It sounds like a good idea.
(O) **Kare wa hijō ni tasai na ningen da.** (E) He's a very gifted person.	(C) **Keredo kare wa kechi na yatsu da.** (M) But he's a very stingy person.
(O) **Senjitsu kare wa shoku o ushinatta sō yo.** (E) The other day I heard he lost his job.	(O) **Kare wa meijitsu aitomonai seiji-tsu na hito na no de zannen da.** (M) Since he's a man of words, it's a pity.

Nigori (゛) And Handaku (゜) Marked Sounds
Basic Kana (ば-Ba) To (ぼ-Bo) Stroke Order

161

Ima kita bakari.
I just came now.

Anata ni bachi ga ataru.
I'll punish you.

Bin o kowashita.
I broke a bottle.

Kare wa binkan desu.
He is sensitive.

Budō o tabete iru.
I'm eating grapes.

Būbū itteita.
He's grumbling.

Benri desu.
It's convenient.

Bekkan ga shimatta.
The annex is closed.

Bōshi o kabutte iru.
He's wearing a cap.

Boku no desu.
It's mine's.

Basic Kana (ば-Ba) To (ぼ-Bo) Stroke Order

FIVE STROKES

Today's Target Kana For Stroke Practice

Last Kana	Hiragana	Katakana	Next Kana
ど	ば	バ	び
DO	Soft Cursive Writing	Stiff Square Strokes	BI

Hints For Stroke Order Reproduction And Recognition

(ば-**ba**), the pronunciation of this kana, is similar to the first sound of the word "barter." For the best stroke writing results, use a felt tip pen. Start from the left and follow the arrows. Using the very first kana as an example, slowly, with a light steady hand, try to accurately form your target kana. Use all blank box spaces and imitate the strokes of your present and last kana until your kana resemble the original ones.

Target Strokes	1	2	3	4	5	6	7	8	9
ば				ば	ば				
バ	ノ	ハ	バ	バ					

THREE STROKES

Last Kana	Today's Target Kana For Stroke Practice		Next Kana
ば	び	ビ	ぶ
	Hiragana Soft Cursive Writing	Katakana Stiff Square Strokes	
BA			BU

Hints For Stroke Order Reproduction And Recognition

(び-**bi**), the pronunciation of this kana, is similar to the first sound of the word "behind." For the best stroke writing results, use a felt tip pen. Start from the left and follow the arrows. Using the very first kana as an example, slowly, with a light steady hand, try to accurately form your target kana. Use all the blank box spaces and imitate the strokes of your present and last kana until your kana resemble the original ones.

Target Strokes	1	2	3	4	5	6	7	8	9
び	び	び	び						
ビ	ノ	ヒ	ビ	ビ					

Basic Kana (ば-Ba) To (ぼ-Bo) Stroke Order

SIX STROKES

Today's Target Kana For Stroke Practice

Last Kana	ぶ	ブ	Next Kana
び	Hiragana Soft Cursive Writing	Katakana Stiff Square Strokes	べ
BI			BE

Hints For Stroke Order Reproduction And Recognition

(ぶ-**bu**), the pronunciation of this kana, is similar to the first sound of the "bu" of the name President George "Bush." For the best stroke writing results, use a felt tip pen. Start from the left and follow the arrows. Using the very first kana as an example, slowly, with a light steady hand, try to accurately form your target kana. Use all the blank box spaces and imitate the strokes of your present and last kana until your kana resemble the original ones.

Target Strokes	1	2	3	4	5	6	7	8	9
ぶ									
ブ									

THREE STROKES

Today's Target Kana For Stroke Practice

Last Kana	Hiragana Soft Cursive Writing	Katakana Stiff Square Strokes	Next Kana
ぶ	べ	ベ	ぼ
BU			BO

Hints For Stroke Order Reproduction And Recognition

(べ-**be**), the pronunciation of this kana, is similar to the first sound of the 'be' in the name "Beverly Hills." For the best stroke writing results, use a felt tip pen. Start from the left and follow the arrows. Using the very first kana as an example, slowly, with a light steady hand, try to accurately form your target kana. Use all the blank box spaces and imitate the strokes of your present and last kana until your kana resemble the original ones.

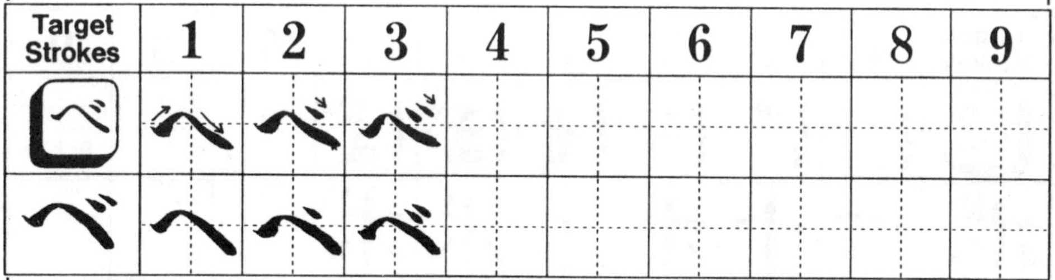

Basic Kana (ば-Ba) To (ぼ-Bo) Stroke Order

SIX STROKES

Today's Target Kana For Stroke Practice

Last Kana: べ (BE)

ぼ — Hiragana Soft Cursive Writing

ボ — Katakana Stiff Square Strokes

Next Kana: ぱ (PA)

Hints For Stroke Order Reproduction And Recognition

(ぼ-**bo**), the pronunciation of this kana, is similar to the first sound of the word "bogus." For the best stroke writing results, use a felt tip pen. Start from the left and follow the arrows. Using the very first kana as an example, slowly, with a light steady hand, try to accurately, form your target kana. Use all the blank box spaces and imitate the strokes of your present and last kana until your kana resemble the original ones.

Target Strokes	1	2	3	4	5	6	7	8	9
ぼ									
ボ									

CREATIVE KANA REVIEW

Write it! Read it! Say it!

ば	び	ぶ	べ	ぼ
BA	BI	BU	BE	BO

LINK-A-LETTER: You have already practiced writing all the hiragana on this page. Now use them to build new words in the adjoining boxes. Then try to link them to phrases.

ばん **ban** evening				べんり **benri** convenient			
ぶらぶら **bura bura** stroll slowly				びん **bin** a bottle			
ぶどう **budō** grape				ばか **baka** a fool			
びんせん **binsen** writing paper				ぼりぼり **bori bori** sound of scratching			
ぶさほう **busahō** bad manners				ばすえ **basue** edge of town			

SEARCH AND MATCH IDENTICAL KANA

Expand your kana recognition ability. Search within the numbers (1-5) for the kana which matches the left hand column Romanized letters. Write the correct kana in the blank boxes. Then use the bottom page boxes to practice any kana you wish.

EXAMPLE:

		Answer	1 ↓	2 ↓	3 ↓	4 ↓	5 ↓
ga	←	3	だ	な	が	み	ぱ

Mark your correct answer numbers in these boxes below			1	2	3	4	5
		↓	↓	↓	↓	↓	↓
ba	←		ぶ	ぼ	ば	べ	び
pi	←		ぴ	ぷ	ぽ	ぺ	ぱ
kya	←		ちょ	きゅ	ちゃ	きゃ	きょ
gu	←		ご	ぐ	ぎ	が	げ
po	←		ぺ	ぽ	ぴ	ぱ	ぷ

Practice writing any kana in these boxes

NATURAL SURVIVAL CONVERSATION

What You Might Hear	How You Might Possibly Answer
(P) **Peiyo-san no otaku desu ka?** (E) Is this the home of Mr. Peiyo?	(VP) **Hai sō de gozaimasu.** (E) Yes, it is.
(P) **Kare o o-negai shimasu.** (E) I'd like to speak to him.	(P) **Dono yō na go-yōken desu ka?** (E) What is your business with him?
(P) **Dōshite watashi ga kare to hanashitai riyu o shiritai no desu ka?** (E) Why do you want to know my reason for wanting to speak to him?	(P) **Kanai desu ga. Shujin wa gaishutsuchū desu.** (W) I'm his wife. He went out.
(P) **Denwa o kudasaru yō tsutaete kudasai. Watashi wa Mihen desu. Denwa bangō wa ni ni nana roku kyū kyū go.** (M) Please tell him to call me. I'm Mihen. My phone number is 227-6995.	(O) **Hai. Wakarimashita. Tsutaemasu.** (VP) **Kashikomarimashita.** (E) I'll tell him.
(O) **Kochira wa Peiyo desu. O-denwa o itadaita sō desu ga.** (E) This is Peiyo. I'm returning your call.	(O) **Yoku kikoemasen.** (E) I can't hear you too well.
(P) **Watashi wa Peiyo to mōshimashita.** (E) I said, "this is Peiyo".	(O) **Kore wa odorokimashita.** (E) What a delightful surprise.
(P) **Moshi moshi, Hadison-san o onegai shitain desu ga.** (E) Hello, I'd like to speak to Mr. Hadison.	(P) **Donna goyōken desu ka?** (E) What's this all about?
(O) **Naimitsu de jūdai na koto desu.** (E) It's very private and very important.	(O) **Watashi ni ienai koto desu ka?** (E) You can't tell me?
(O) **Kaisha no himitsu wa akasemasen.** (E) I never divulge company secrets.	(O) **Kikō to wa yume ni mo omotte imasen.** (E) I wouldn't dream of asking you.

170

Vocabulary Expanding For Interacting

Getting Your Telephone Message Across

NATURAL SURVIVAL CONVERSATION

What You Might Hear	How You Might Possibly Answer
(O) **Kare wa imasu ka, soretomo imasen-ka?** (M) Is he in or out?	(P) **Ima kare wa gaishutsuchū desu.** (E) He's out right now.
(O) **Naze sugu shirase naino?** (W) Why didn't you tell me sooner?	(P) **Sugu otsutae dekizu ni sumimasen.** (E) I regret this unfortunate delay.
(C) **Denwa ga kakatte imasu yo.** (E) You have an incoming call.	(O) **Hai. Wakatte-imasu. Kyatchihon ga tsukaemasu.** (E) Yes, I know. My catchphone is in operation.

DOODLE **Fun With Hiragana Combinations**

AS ON OTHER PAGES, THESE MOSTLY MEANINGLESS COMBINATIONS OF SOUNDS WHOSE LETTERS ARE DRAWN SO THAT THEY RESEMBLE HUMAN FACES. THEY PROVIDE YOU A GOOD ARMCHAIR HOBBY MIMICKING WRITING KANA IDEOGRAMS FOR PRACTICE PURPOSES.

いけいけしこく

Go to Shikoku.

××たべすぎ

Don't eat too much.

まいこさん

The Maiko girl

つるムし二八〇〇

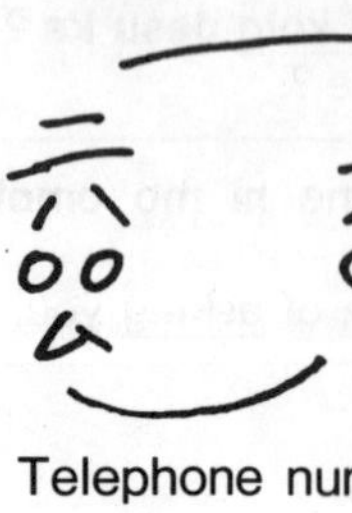

Telephone number 280064

しめしめとんび

I'm lucky.

しめんそか

Surrounded by opponents

Contracted Sounds With One Dot
Basic Kana (ぱ-Pa) To (ぽ-Po) Stroke Order

171

Pāma o kakeru.
I'm getting a perm.

Pari-pari taberu.
Munching with a crunchy sound.

Puro kaomake.
Just like a professional.

Pun-pun okoru.
Very upset.

Pittari na pantsu.
Tight fitting pants.

Piiman wa kirai.
I don't like green peppers.

Pera-pera shaberu.
Chatter incessantly.

Peko-peko suru.
Bowing constantly.

Pokkuri shinda.
Died suddenly.

Ponto oto ga suru.
Make a bouncing sound.

Basic kana (ぱ-Pa) To (ぽ-Po) Stroke Order

FOUR STROKES

Today's Target Kana For Stroke Practice

Last Kana	Hiragana	Katakana	Next Kana
ぼ	ぱ	パ	ぴ
BO	Hiragana Soft Cursive Writing	Katakana Stiff Square Strokes	PI

Hints For Stroke Order Reproduction And Recognition

(ぱ-**pa**), the pronunciation of this kana, is similar to the first sound of the word "papa." For the best stroke writing results, use a felt tip pen. Start from the left and follow the arrows. Using the very first kana as an example, slowly, with a light steady hand, try to accurately form your target kana. Use all the blank box spaces and imitate the strokes of your present and last kana until your kana resemble the original ones.

Target Strokes	1	2	3	4	5	6	7	8	9
ぱ									
パ									

TWO STROKES

Today's Target Kana For Stroke Practice

Last Kana	Hiragana Soft Cursive Writing	Katakana Stiff Square Strokes	Next Kana
ぱ	ぴ	ピ	ぷ
PA			PU

Hints For Stroke Order Reproduction And Recognition

(ぴ-**pi**), the pronunciation of this kana, is similar to the first sound of the word "piano." For the best stroke writing results, use a felt tip pen. Start from the left and follow the arrows. Using the very first kana as an example, slowly, with a light steady hand, try to accurately form your target kana. Use all the blank box spaces and imitate the strokes of your present and last kana until your kana resemble the original ones.

Target Strokes	1	2	3	4	5	6	7	8	9
ぴ	ひ	ぴ							
ピ	ノ	ヒ	ピ						

FIVE STROKES

Today's Target Kana For Stroke Practice

Last Kana	Hiragana Soft Cursive Writing	Katakana Stiff Square Strokes	Next Kana
ぴ	ぷ	プ	ぺ
PI			PE

Hints For Stroke Order Reproduction And Recognition

(ぷ-**pu**), the pronunciation of this kana, is similar to the first sound of the word "pushy." For the best stroke writing results, use a felt tip pen. Start from the left and follow the arrows. Using the very first kana as an example, slowly, with a light steady hand, try to accurately form your target kana. Use all the blank box spaces and imitate the strokes of your present and last kana until your kana resemble the original ones.

Target Strokes	1	2	3	4	5	6	7	8	9
ぷ									
プ	フ	プ							

TWO STROKES

Today's Target Kana For Stroke Practice

Last Kana	Hiragana Soft Cursive Writing	Katakana Stiff Square Strokes	Next Kana
ぷ	ぺ	ペ	ぽ
PU			PO

Hints For Stroke Order Reproduction And Recognition

(ぺ-**pe**), the pronunciation of this kana, is similar to the first sound of the French bottled sparkling mineral water "Perrier." For the best stroke writing results, use a felt tip pen. Start from the left and follow the arrows. Using the very first kana as an example, slowly, with a light steady hand, try to accurately form your target kana. Use all the blank box spaces and imitate the strokes of your present and last kana until your kana resemble the original ones.

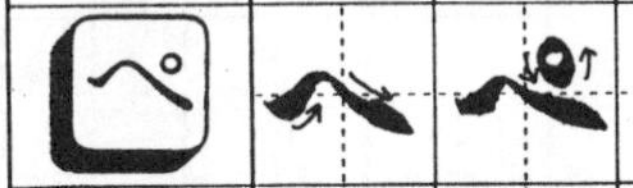

Target Strokes	1	2	3	4	5	6	7	8	9
ぺ	へ	ぺ							

FIVE STROKES

Today's Target Kana For Stroke Practice

Last Kana			Next Kana
ぺ	ぽ	ポ	きゃ
PE	Hiragana Soft Cursive Writing	Katakana Stiff Square Strokes	KYA

Hints For Stroke Order Reproduction And Recognition

(ぽ-**po**), the pronunciation of this kana, is similar to the first sound of the card game "Poker." For the best stroke writing results, use a felt tip pen. Start from the left and follow the arrows. Using the very first kana as an example, slowly, with a light steady hand, try to accurately form your target kana. Use all the blank box spaces and imitate the strokes of your present and last kana until your kana resemble the original ones.

Target Strokes	1	2	3	4	5	6	7	8	9

CREATIVE KANA REVIEW

Write it! Read it! Say it!

ぱ	ぴ	ぷ	ぺ	ぽ
PA	PI	PU	PE	PO

LINK-A-LETTER: You have already practiced writing all the hiragana on this page. Now use them to build new words in the adjoining boxes. Then try to link them to phrases.

ぴりぴり **piri piri** nervous				ぴんぴん **pin pin** fresh and strong			
ぺてん **peten** trickery				ぱん **pan** bread			
ぶんぷ **bunpu** distribution				ぽけっと **poketto** pocket			
てっぽう **teppō** gun, rifle				ぱちんこ **pachinko** pinball			
ぺらぺら **pera pera** good at				ぷんぷん **pun pun** fumming			

178 SEARCH AND MATCH IDENTICAL KANA

Expand your kana recognition ability. Search within the numbers (1-5) for the kana which matches the left hand column Romanized letters. Write the correct kana in the blank boxes. Then use the bottom page boxes to practice any kana you wish.

EXAMPLE:

		Answer	1	2	3	4	5
			↓	↓	↓	↓	↓
ga	←	3	だ	な	が	み	ぱ

Mark your correct answer numbers in these boxes below			1	2	3	4	5
		↓	↓	↓	↓	↓	↓
kya	←		きゅ	きゃ	しゃ	きょ	しゃ
na	←		お	ほ	な	は	ぼ
kyo	←		しゃ	きょ	ちゃ	きゅ	きゃ
me	←		て	の	め	む	り
n	←		や	ん	え	れ	ま

Practice writing any kana in these boxes

Combined Kana Sound Changes
Basic Kana (きゃ-Kya) To (きょ-Kyo) Stroke Order

Kyaku ga kita.
A customer has come.

Kodomo ga kyā-kyā sawagu.
The children are screaming.

Sore wa kyū-sugiru.
It's very urgent.

Kyūkyūsha ga kita.
The ambulance has come.

Kyōkai wa moeta.
The church burned down.

Inkyo seikatsu o suru.
He's enjoying retirement.

Basic Kana (きゃ-Kya) To (きょ-Kyo) Stroke Order

SEVEN STROKES

Today's Target Kana For Stroke Practice

Last Kana	Hiragana Soft Cursive Writing	Katakana Stiff Square Strokes	Next Kana
ぽ	きゃ	キャ	きゅ
PO			KYU

Hints For Stroke Order Reproduction And Recognition

(きゃ-**kya**), the pronunciation of this kana, is similar to the first sound of the Sri Lankan city, "Kandy." For the best stroke writing results, use a felt tip pen. Start from the left and follow the arrows. Using the very first kana as an example, slowly, with a light steady hand, try to accurately form your target kana. Use all the blank box spaces and imitate the strokes of your present and last kana until your kana resemble the original ones.

Target Strokes	1	2	3	4	5	6	7	8	9
きゃ									
キャ	ー	ニ	キ						

FIVE STROKES

Today's Target Kana For Stroke Practice

Last Kana			Next Kana
きゃ	きゅ	キュ	きょ
KYA	Hiragana Soft Cursive Writing	Katakana Stiff Square Strokes	KYO

Hints For Stroke Order Reproduction And Recognition

(きゅ-**kyu**), the pronunciation of this kana, is similar to the first sound of the word "cubic." For the best stroke writing results, use a felt tip pen. Start from the left and follow the arrows. Using the very first kana as an example, slowly, with a light steady hand, try to accurately form your target kana. Use all the blank box spaces and imitate the strokes of your present and last kana until your kana resemble the original ones.

Target Strokes	1	2	3	4	5	6	7	8	9
きゅ									
キュ	ー	ニ	キ		キュ				

Basic Kana (きゃ-Kya) To (きょ-Kyo) Stroke Order

SIX STROKES

Today's Target Kana For Stroke Practice

Last Kana	Hiragana Soft Cursive Writing	Katakana Stiff Square Strokes	Next Kana
きゅ	きょ	キョ	しゃ
KYU			SHA

Hints For Stroke Order Reproduction And Recognition

(きょ-**kyo**), the pronunciation of this kana, is similar to the first sound of the word "clone." For the best stroke writing results, use a felt tip pen. Start from the left and follow the arrows. Using the very first kana as an example, slowly, with a light steady hand, try to accurately form your target kana. Use all the blank box spaces and imitate the strokes of your present and last kana until your kana resemble the original ones.

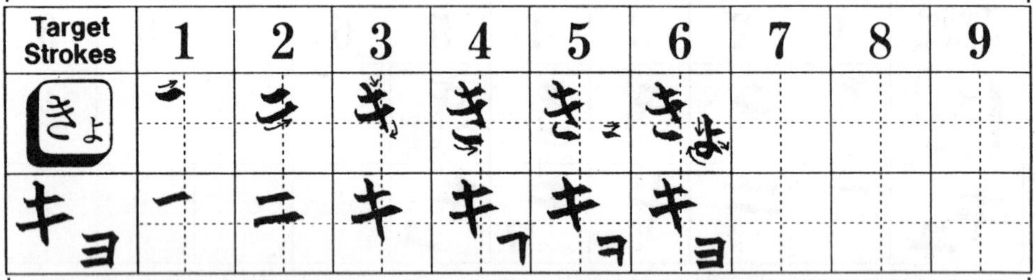

Basic Kana (きゃ-Kya) To (きょ-Kyo) Stroke Order

CREATIVE KANA REVIEW

Write it! Read it! Say it!

きゃ		きゅ		きょ
KYA		KYU		KYO

LINK-A-LETTER: You have already practiced writing all the hiragana on this page. Now use them to build new words in the adjoining boxes. Then try to link them to phrases.

きょうい **kyōi** amazing				きょうみ **kyōmi** hobby			
きゃく **kyaku** customer				きょう **kyō** today			
きょく **kyoku** a song				きょうふ **kyōfu** fear			
きょねん **kyonen** last year				きょり **kyori** distance			
きゅうか **kyūka** vacation				きょひ **kyohi** refuse			

184 Basic Steps To Forming Japanese Sentences

Your purpose in learning to write and read Japanese kana is, naturally, to communicate with Japanese citizens. In the process of learning to write, the best way to memorize kana is not merely by the individual ideograms but in words and sentences. But in order to properly write words and sentences you have to know how to go about constructing sentences which make sense. We feel we would not be helping you to attain your goal if we neglected to help you in this respect. So we've set down a few pointers as 'food for thought', which you can fall back on if you ever get in a tight spot. And you will !

Explanation of Particles

The nuance of a sentence, as well as its forms, is controlled by particles, which in themselves do not have the perfect meanings that prepositions do in English. A particle is an auxiliary to other words in a sentence. However, the particle, which is peculiar to Japanese grammar, is very important in Japanese speech. If a particle is not used, verbally or in writing, the sentence will become stilted and grammatically imperfect.

The main problem most non-Japanese learners of Japanese have to face is not so much pronunciation, but knowing which words go where in sentence construction, how one is supposed to know which word to place before the other and even which word to place at the beginning of a sentence. An additional problem is, how one can distinguish between the duties of the particles **wa** and **ga**, which are valuable 'suffixes' to nouns and pronouns used in the nominative case.

Called **joshi** in Japanese, these two **kana** are the ones most frequently placed next to a Chinese ideograph in any written material to show its Japanese deflection. Their uses are very simple. Remember that whenever you want to say 'as for something' or 'as for mister so and so' (that is, when referring to a person or thing), as a rule you'd use **wa**, which is a 'topic marker'. When making a negative sentence, 99% of the time you'd use **wa** instead of **ga**. Also remember that whenever you want to imply 'and' or 'but', as a rule you'd use **ga**. **Ga** shows a subject. It can be used with the subject when it has the meaning of 'there is' when implying 'something can be done', and when someone 'desires' something. **Ga** introduces a related statement, connects two sentences because it emphasizes an immediate subject, and focuses on the word which comes before it. You'd express the nominative case by attaching **wa** and **ga** after a noun.

The following pertinent points for sentence forming are necessary to know because they emphasize the basic differences between the grammar of your mother tongue and Japanese grammar.

1) Although the plural of certain words can be expressed through the use of a suffix, Japanese nouns are neither gender or number specific.
2) A sentence always begins with a subject and generally ends with a verb. The object is normally found in the middle as you will notice when you read the various examples of sentences.
3) The role of a particle is as important to Japanese grammar as the preposition is to English. A sentence never begins with a particle, which, for the the most part follows a noun, verb or adjective.

Examples: **America ni** ... (In America ....)
Mayowanai de ... (Don't get lost)

4) Adjectives have several functions. They can modify a subsequent noun: **takai hon** (expensive book), show present and past; **takakatta** (was expensive), and affirmative **nurui** (is lukewarm) and negative, **arimasen** (there isn't any).
5) Verb conjugation shows the present and past form of tenses and does not distinguish between gender or the number of persons of a subject.
6) Several degrees of politeness can be expressed with Japanese verbs. Be sure to notice the bracketed letter next to the Japanese survival conversation sentences indicating their degree of politeness. This is explained in the book layout explanation section.

The following are a few sample sentences broken down to show their construction, so that you can refer back to them and also construct sentences in a systematic way.

186 Basic Steps To Forming Japanese Sentences

—Sentence Formation Guidelines—

In a normal sentence (non-comparative sentence using pronouns), the object comes first. If there is an adverb, then it follows, and finally the verb ends the sentence.

So in a regular Japanese sentence, the main working essence is : 1) subject, 2) adverb, 3) object, and 4) verb.

Before you study the breakdown of a sentence, first notice the workings of the particles, which give sense to a sentence.

Example :

Watashi **wa** **hana** **ga** **suki desu**.
(I) [particle] (flowers) [particle] (like)

"Wa" belongs to "**Watashi**" and "**ga**" belongs to "**hana**".
(I like flowers.)

Watashi **wa** **Tokyo** **ni** **tsukimashita**.
(I) [particle] (at) (arrived)

"**Wa**" belongs to "**Watashi**" and "**ni**" belongs to "Tokyo".
(I arrived at Tokyo.)

And now, notice the various specimen sentences.

Example No. 1

Kinō hon o kaimashita.

[adverb]	[direct object]	[particle showing object]	[verb]
Kinō	**hon**	**o**	**kaimashita**
Yesterday	book		bought

(I bought a book yesterday.)

*In most sentences personal pronouns are omitted.

Example No. 2

In a comparative sentence, first comes the subject (I, you, it, etc.), next the object, adverb, and then the verb.

[subject]	[particle]	[adverb]	[direct object]
Watashi	**wa**	**kinō**	**hon**

[particle showing the object]	(verb)
o	**kaimashita.**

Watashi wa kinō hon o kaimashita.
I bought a book yesterday.
*__Wa__ is used to emphasize or refer to 'watashi'.
This sentence emphasizes who the buyer is, which in this case is 'I'.
**As a rule the first two examples of sentence styles are used more than 70% of the time. But in actual speaking, there'll be many exceptions.

Example No. 3

personal pronoun	particle	personal pronoun	particle	adverb	adjective	auxiliary verb
Kare	**wa**	**watashi**	**o**	**tottemo**	**okora-**	**seta**
He		me		very	get angry	made.
subject		object		modifier		

He made me get very angry.

Example No. 4:

1	2	3	4
Watashi	**wa**	**ha-isha**	**desu.**
I		dentist	am.

1) Subject
3) Compliment
4) Verb

2) Special particle which shows a subject like "**ga**". It is included in 'I', 'you', and other English personal pronouns.

I am a dentist.

Example No. 5:

1	2	3	4
[subject]	[particle]	[object]	[verb]
Kare	**wa**	**Kaimono ni**	**ikimashita**
He		shopping	went.

He went shopping.

Basic Steps To Forming Japanese Sentences

Adjective case

1	2	3	4	5
[subject]	[adverb]	[adjective]	[noun]	[verb]
Anata wa	**totemo**	**kirei na**	**me o**	**shite iru**
You	very	pretty	eyes	have.

You have very pretty eyes.

(O)				
	[subject]	[object]	[noun]	[particle]
	Kare wa	**watashi ni**	**kare**	**no**
	He	me	his	

[noun object]	[particle]	[verb]	[verb]
kuruma	**o**	**tsukawasete**	**kureta.**
car		use	let.

He let me use his car.

[personal pronoun]	[particle]	[personal pronoun]	[noun]	[particle]
Watashi	**wa**	**watashi no**	**fuku**	**o**
I		my	clothes	
[subject]		[modifier]	[object]	

[verb]
araitai.
want to wash.
[predicate verb]

I want to wash my clothes.

1	2	3	4
[subject]	[adverb]	[object]	[verb]
kare wa	**wazato**	**watashi o**	**oshita**
He	on purpose	me	bumped.

He bumped me on purpose.

NATURAL SURVIVAL CONVERSATION

What You Might Hear	How You Might Possibly Answer
(P) **Sore wa yoroshii desu ka?** (E) Is that alright?	(O) **Hai, daijōbu desu.** *(or)* **Daijōbu desu.** (E) Yes, it's alright. *(or)* It's alright.
(P) **Daijōbu desu ka?** (E) Are you alright?	(P) **Daijōbu desu.** (W) I'm alright.
(C) **Iya.** (W) I don't like it.	(P) **Sō na no.** (W) I see.
(P) **Watashi-tachi dake no hanashi desu.** (E) Just between the two of us.	(P) **Himitsu wa hanasu-koto ga dekimasen.** (E) We don't share any secrets.
(O) **Kare wa hakkiri ii sugiru.** (E) He's too frank.	(O) **Kare wa mizukusai.** (E) I don't think he's frank enough.
(O) **Fun-iki o akaruku shita.** (E) He brightened the atmosphere.	(O) **Kare no ie no o-tetsudai-san wa inki na hito da.** (E) But his housegirl is a gloom-merchant.
(O) **Itsu doko ka wakaranai ga doko ka e okane o otoshita.** (E) I don't know when or where but I lost my money.	(O) **Anata no oku-san ga nusunda kanōsei mo aru deshō.** (E) Could your wife have stolen it?
(O) **Kare wa on shirazu desu.** *(or)* **Giri shirazu.** (E) He doesn't know how to take care of his obligations.	(O) **Sono tōri desu. Watashi no kotoba o shinji nasai.** (E) He does. Take my word for it.
(O) **Shinpuku-san wa jisatsu-suru mae hara-ippai tabemashita.** (E) Mr. Shinpuku satisfied himself before committing suicide.	(O) **Kare wa shotai-mochi desu.** (E) He's a family man.
(C) **Nanika hoshii mono wa nai ka?** (M) Isn't there anything you want?	(O) **Iie, nani mo irimasen.** (E) No. I don't need anything.

190

Vocabulary Expanding For Interacting

Expressing Mixed Emotions

NATURAL SURVIVAL CONVERSATION

What You Might Hear	How You Might Possibly Answer
(P) **Shūmatsu wa dono yō ni osugoshi desu ka?** (E) How have you been spending your free time on weekends?	(O) **Manga no zasshi o nansatsu mo yonda.** (E) I've read a lot of comic books.
(O) **Boku wa paku-paku oto tatete nan demo itadakimasu.** (M) I eat most everything noisily with my mouth open.	(O) **Kono uchi dewa shizuka ni soshite jōhin ni shokuji shimasu.** (E) In this house we eat quietly and with grace.
(C) **Kare wa kaisha no kane o ōryō shita.** (E) He embezzled the company's money.	(O) **Sonna koto wa sōzō mo tsukimasendeshita.** (E) I couldn't imagine such a thing.
(P) **Umibe wa kirei dato omoimasu ka?** (E) Do you think the beach is clean?	(P) **Sumimasen. Eigo de henji ga dekimasen.** (E) I'm sorry I can't answer you in English.
(C) **Dewa mata.** (E) Well, till next time.	(O) **Yoroshiku o-negai shimasu.** (E) Treat me favorably.
(P) **Arigatō gozaimasu.** (E) Thank you very much.	(P) **Dō itashimashite.** (E) Don't mention it.
(O) **Anata o machi no sumizumi made sagashimashita.** (E) I looked for you on every street corner in your town.	(O) **En ga nakatta to omotte akirameru.** (E) It wouldn't have worked anyway so forget it.
(O) **Inu ga kyan-kyan naite iru.** (E) The dog is yelping.	(C) **Watashi wa kono inu ni nare chatta.** (E) I've grown accustomed to this dog.

Combined Kana Sound Changes
Basic Kana (しゃ-Sha) To (しょ-Sho) Stroke Order

Shakan kyori o toru.
Keep your distance between cars.

Shaberu na!
Don't speak!

Oyome-san to uma wa shan-shan to oto tateru.
The bride and the horse make a shimmying sound.

Shūdensha ni nori okureta.
I missed the last train.

Shūkanshi o kaitai.
I want to buy a weekly magazine.

Sore wa mata to nai kikai desu. Zehi shutsuen sasete kudasai.
That would be the chance of a lifetime. I'd love to.

Shōshō desu.
It isn't much.

Shōkai shite kureru?
Can you introduce me?

Shokuji ni shōtai shitai.
I want to invite you to dinner.

FOUR STROKES

Today's Target Kana For Stroke Practice

Last Kana	Hiragana Soft Cursive Writing	Katakana Stiff Square Strokes	Next Kana
きょ	しゃ	シャ	しゅ
KYO			SHU

Hints For Stroke Order Reproduction And Recognition

(しゃ-**sha**), the pronunciation of this kana, is similar to the first sound of the word "shadow". For the best stroke writing results, use a felt tip pen. Start from the left and follow the arrows. Using the very first kana as an example, slowly, with a light steady hand, try to accurately form your target kana. Use all the blank box spaces and imitate the strokes of your present and last kana until your kana resemble the original ones.

Target Strokes	1	2	3	4	5	6	7	8	9
しゃ	し	しっ	しゃ	しゃ					
シャ	ヽ	ミ	シ	シっ	シャ				

TWO STROKES

Today's Target Kana For Stroke Practice

Last Kana	Hiragana Soft Cursive Writing	Katakana Stiff Square Strokes	Next Kana
しゃ	しゅ	シュ	しょ
SHA			SHO

Hints For Stroke Order Reproduction And Recognition

(しゅ-**shu**), the pronunciation of this kana, is similar to the first sound of the word "shoe." For the best stroke writing results, use a felt tip pen. Start from the left and follow the arrows. Using the very first kana as an example, slowly, with a light steady hand, try to accurately form your target kana. Use all the blank box spaces and imitate the strokes of your present and last kana until your kana resemble the original ones.

Target Strokes	1	2	3	4	5	6	7	8	9
しゅ	し	しゅ							
シュ	ヽ	ミ	シ	シ¬	シュ				

Basic Kana (しゃ-Sha) To (しょ-Sho) Stroke Order

THREE STROKES

Today's Target Kana For Stroke Practice

Last Kana			Next Kana
しゅ	しょ	ショ	ちゃ
SHU	Hiragana Soft Cursive Writing	Katakana Stiff Square Strokes	CHA

Hints For Stroke Order Reproduction And Recognition

(しょ-**sho**), the pronunciation of this kana, is similar to the first sound of the word "show". For the best stroke writing results, use a felt tip pen. Start from the left and follow the arrows. Using the very first kana as example, slowly, with a light steady hand, try to accurately form your target kana. Use all the blank box spaces and imitate the strokes of your present and last kana until your kana resemble the original ones.

Target Strokes	1	2	3	4	5	6	7	8	9
しょ	し	しょ	しょ						
ショ	丶	〃	シ	シ	ショ	ショ			

Basic Kana (しゃ-Sha) To (しょ-Sho) Stroke Order

CREATIVE KANA REVIEW
Write it! Read it! Say it!

しゃ		しゅ		しょ
SHA		SHU		SHO

LINK-A-LETTER: You have already practiced writing all the hiragana on this page. Now use them to build new words in the adjoining boxes. Then try to link them to phrases.

しゃれ **share** a joke				しゃこ **shako** garage			
しゅみ **shumi** hobby				しゃぶしゃぶ **shabu shabu** sliced boiled meat			
しゃいん **shain** company personnel				しゅうまつ **shūmatsu** weekend			
しょうばい **shōbai** business				しゅうかん **shūkan** weekly			
しゃちょう **shachō** boss				しょう **shō** a prize			

196 Adverbial Particles (Fuku-joshi)

Particles of this category are combined with various parts of speech and function as adverbial modifiers, thus they are referred to as adverbial particles.

だけ

The particle (**dake**-だけ) indicates that the means or action expressed is singularly restricted to it and never extends beyond it.
Example :
(O) **Watashi wa shimbun dake de shitta.**
(E) I knew about it only through the newspapers.

ほど

The particle (**hodo**-ほど) indicates an approximation of number, or sometimes degree.
Example :
(O) **Waku-waku suru hodo ureshii.**
(E) I'm so happy, that my heart is pounding.

まで

The particle (**made**-まで), which means 'up to', expresses the finalization of an action or the extent to which an action will be performed. It also means 'as far as' or 'until.'
Example :
(O) **Shibu-shibu koko made kita.**
(E) I came here complaining all my way.

くらい

(**kurai**-くらい) is a particle expressing a rough estimate or approximation. It is considered more colloquial than the particle 'hodo'.
Example :
(O) **Atama ga gan-gan suru kurai itai.**
(E) I have a splitting headache.

ばかり

The particle (**bakari**-ばかり) expresses the cause or duration of time or length.
Example :
(O) **Musha-musha tabete bakari iru.**
(E) I'm now munching on some grass.

Interrogative Particles (**gimon-joshi**)

か

The particle (**ka-か**), used at the end of a sentence, turns it into an interrogative sentence. Its inclusion at the end of a sentence does not require any change in the word order. The presence of **'ka'** in a sentence makes it interrogative regardless of the presence or absence of other interrogative words. As in other languages, the Japanese language employs rising intonations in order to change a declarative sentence into an interrogative one. In some cases where the intonation and situation makes an interrogative sentence obvious, the particle 'ka' definitely is omitted.

Examples :

(O) **Dōshite boku ni iwanakatta-n-da ?**
(M) Why didn't you tell me ?

(P) **Kono resutoran wa dō kashira ?**
(E) What do you think of this restaurant ?

Interjections (**kantōshi**)

さ

(sa-さ) This suffix, being an intensifier rather than an interjectional, emphatically draws the listener's attention to words to which it is attached.

Example :

(O) **Sā, soro-soro shuppatsu shiyō.**
(E) It's just about time to depart.

ね

(**ne-ね**) Used when the speaker is soliciting the listener's consent, this suffix usually expresses sympathy or agreement.

Examples :

(C) **Ne, gatsu-gatsu shinai de !**
(E) Say, don't be so greedy !

(O) **Otagai ni ki ga togamete itan desu ne.**
(E) We're both feeling guilty.

な

(na-な) Normally combined with the adjective '**no ni**', this suffix expresses pleasure or a pleasant surprise. It can also be used to forbid a particular behavior.
Example :
(C) **Ira-ira suru na !**
(E) Don't get irritated !

よ

(yo-よ) This suffix indicates exhortation or a strong emotion.
Examples :
(O) **Niko-niko shiro yo !**
(E) Keep on smiling !

(C) **Sassoku ikō yo !**
(E) Let's go soon !

* * * * * **Notes on Pronouns** * * * * *

Personal pronouns, especially first person pronouns, are usually omitted as much as possible in Japanese conversation, except to make it perfectly clear who's referring to whom or to what.
Example : (O) **Jimusho e ikimasu.**
(E) I'm going to the office.

If you prefer to use pronouns, you'd simply place them at the beginning of a sentence.
Example : (O) **Kanojo wa byōki desu.**
(E) She's sick.

It's only necessary to use pronouns when omitting them might cause confusion.
(O) **Kare wa Rahendi de watashi wa Paburo desu.**
(E) He's Rahendi and I'm Pablo.

NATURAL SURVIVAL CONVERSATION

What You Might Hear	How You Might Possibly Answer
(C) **Chotto anata wa Rumgo-san dewa arimasen ka?** (E) Say, aren't you Mr. Rumgo?	(O) **Mada sono namae o tsukatte imasu.** (E) That's still the name I use.
(C) **Megane kakete inai toki ni anata ni nita hito ni dekuwashita.** (E) I bumped into someone who looked like you, when I didn't have my glassen on.	(M) **Boku janakatta. Sore kara dō natta ka?** (E) It wasn't me. Well, what happened then?
(O) **Suru to suri dato wakatta.** (E) Whereupon I recognized him as a pickpocket.	(M) **Soshite dōshita?** (E) And then what did you do?
(O) **Kare ga shiranai uchi ni saifu o torimodoshita.** (E) I retrieved my wallet from him, without him even knowing it.	(C) **Sō shitara ichimai uwate da ne!** (M) If that's the case you're a better man than him.
(O) **Sore demo anzensei to yū koto o itsumo kangaemasu.** (E) Nonetheless, I always think safety.	(O) **Sonna toki yūki ga attara onaji koto o shita deshō.** (E) In that case if I had guts I'd have done the same thing.
(O) **Keredomo watashi no mane wa dare ni mo susume masen.** (E) However I don't advise anyone to follow my example.	(O) **Soko de poketto ni chakku o nui-tsukemasu.** (E) Well then, I'll sew zippers into my pockets.
(P) **Dewa shitsurei itashimasu.** (E) Well then, I'll say goodbye now.	(O) **Demo watashi-tachi wa atta bakari desu.** (E) But we just met.

200 Combined Kana Sound Changes
Basic Kana (ちゃ-Cha) To (ちょ-Cho) Stroke Order

Jimen wa chairo da.
The earth is brown.

Chakku ga kowareta.
My zipper is broken.

Chanto suwaru!
Sit up straight!

Chūcho suru na!
Don't hesitate!

Chūi suru.
Be attentive.

Oobune ni notta tsumori de nan demo chūmon shite kudasai.
Sit back, relax. I'll take care of everything. Order whatever you like.

Chōkai menshoku ni natta.
He was red-faced.

Chokin o shita.
I opened a bank account.

FIVE STROKES

Today's Target Kana For Stroke Practice

Last Kana			Next Kana
しょ	ちゃ	チャ	ちゅ
SHO	Hiragana Soft Cursive Writing	Katakana Stiff Square Strokes	CHU

Hints For Stroke Order Reproduction And Recognition

(ちゃ-**Cha**), the pronunciation of this kana, is similar in sound to the dance word "cha cha", when pronounced rapidly. For the best stroke writing results, use a felt tip pen. Start from the left and follow the arrows. Using the very first kana as an example, slowly, with a light steady hand, try to accurately form your target kana. Use all the blank box spaces and imitate the strokes of your present and last kana until your kana resemble the original ones.

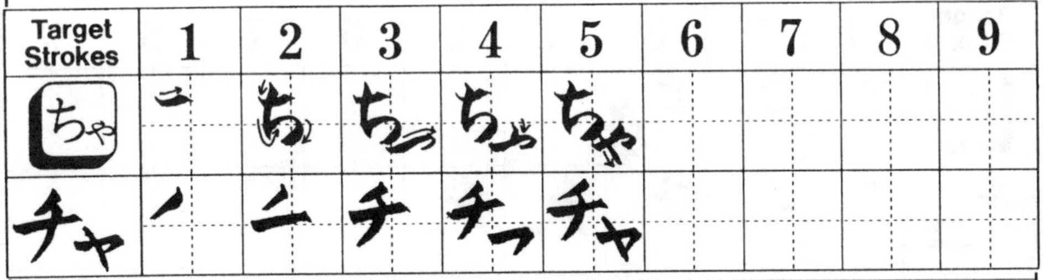

THREE STROKES

Today's Target Kana For Stroke Practice

Last Kana	Hiragana	Katakana	Next Kana
ちゃ	ちゅ	チュ	ちょ
CHA	Hiragana Soft Cursive Writing	Katakana Stiff Square Strokes	CHO

Hints For Stroke Order Reproduction And Recognition

(ちゅ-**chu**), the pronunciation of this kana, is similar to "choo" of the American word "choo-choo-train", when pronounced rapidly. For the best stroke writing results, use a felt tip pen. Then start from the left and follow the arrows. Using the very first kana as an example, slowly, with a light steady hand, try to accurately form your target kana. Use all the blank box spaces and imitate the strokes of your present and last kana until your kana resemble the original ones.

Target Strokes	1	2	3	4	5	6	7	8	9
ちゅ			ちゅ						
チュ	ノ	ニ	チ		チュ				

FOUR STROKES

Today's Target Kana For Stroke Practice

Last Kana			Next Kana
ちゅ	ちょ	チョ	にゃ
CHU	Hiragana Soft Cursive Writing	Katakana Stiff Square Strokes	NYA

Hints For Stroke Order Reproduction And Recognition

(ちょ-**cho**), the pronunciation of this kana, is similar in sound to the first sound of the word "chocolate", when spoken rapidly. For the best stroke writing results, use a felt tip pen. Then start from the left and follow the arrows. Using the very first kana as an example, slowly, with a light steady hand, try to accurately form your target kana. Use all the blank box spaces and imitate the strokes of your present and last kana until your kana resemble the original ones.

Target Strokes	1	2	3	4	5	6	7	8	9
ちょ	⼀	ち	ちょ	ちょ					
チョ	ノ	ニ	チ	チ	チョ	チョ			

Basic Kana (ちゃ-Cha) To (ちょ-Cho) Stroke Order

CREATIVE KANA REVIEW
Write it! Read it! Say it!

ちゃ		ちゅ		ちょ
CHA		CHU		CHO

LINK-A-LETTER: You have already practiced writing all the hiragana on this page. Now use them to build new words in the adjoining boxes. Then try to link them to phrases.

ちゃ **cha** tea				ちゃんと **chanto** neatly			
ちゅう **chū** middle				ちょうし **chōshi** mood			
ちゃわん **chawan** cup				ちょう **chō** district			
ちょうめ **chōme** street				ちょうど **chōdo** precisely			
ちゅうい **chūi** warning				ちゅうごく **Chūgoku** China (country)			

SEARCH FOR THE CORRECT SENTENCES THESE WORDS COME FROM. THEN, INCLUDING THESE WORDS, WRITE THE COMPLETE SENTENCES IN HIRAGANA. MAKE SURE THEY ARE PROPERLY WRITTEN AND SPACED. THEN READ THEM ALL ALOUD FOR PRONUNCIATION PRACTICE.

Vocabulary Expanding For Interacting

Showing Intentions Plus Using Colors

NATURAL SURVIVAL CONVERSATION

What You Might Hear	How You Might Possibly Answer
(O) **Ashita watashi wa kasshoku no ko-inu o kau tsumori desu.** (E) Tomorrow, I intend to buy a tan puppy.	(O) **Inu ga wan-wan hoetara nemure nai deshō.** (E) You'll not sleep if a dog barks 'bow wow'.
(O) **Eiga o miyō to omotte iru keredo naka-naka ikarenai.** (E) I'm thinking of seeing a movie but I can't afford to go.	(O) **Yūbinya-san ga ton-ton to doa o nokku shita.** (E) The mailman knocked on the door.
(P) **Kinō doko e o-dekake deshita ka ?** (E) Where did you go yesterday ?	(O) **Kuroi kutsu o kai ni itta.** (E) I went to buy a pair of black shoes.
(O) **Oodan-hodō o watarō !** (M) Let's cross at the pedestrian crossing !	(O) **Hora ! Hora! Ano shiro to pinku-iro no zubon o haita onna ga niya-niya shite iru.** (M) Look ! Look ! That girl wearing white and pink pants is grinning more and more.
(O) **Kare wa kekkon suru rashii.** (E) It seems he's getting married.	(O) **Kare ni iro no tsuite-nai gurasu o oiwai ni agemashō.** (E) Let's give him non-tinted glasses as a wedding gift.
(O) **Kin-iro no bakku o tsukurasemashita.** (E) I had a gold handbag made.	(O) **Shikashi gin-iro no o tsukuraseru beki datta.** (E) You should have had a silver one made.
(O) **Cha-iro ni someta hazu na no ni.** (E) I thought it was dyed brown.	(O) **Kuyo-kuyo shinai koto ni shita.** (E) I decided not to bother myself about it.
(O) **Kono beiju-iro no denwa yori zōge iro no hō ga motto ii.** (E) An ivory colored telephone looks better than this beige colored one.	(O) **Atchi no denwa mo waruku-nai.** (E) That telephone is not bad.

NATURAL SURVIVAL CONVERSATION

What You Might Hear	How You Might Possibly Answer
(O) **Tomodachi ga aoiro to midori-iro no kiji o sagasu no o tetsudatte kureta.** (E) My friend helped me to find some blue and green material.	(O) **Kare wa shiba-shiba tetsudatte kuremasu ka ?** (E) Does he help you often ?
(C) **Murasaki-iro no furoshiki wa nihon dewa engi ga ii to omoware te iru.** (E) A purple colored wrapping-cloth is considered lucky in Japan.	(O) **Sore o omiyage toshite uketoru no o kotowari-taku-nai ga kotowatta.** (E) I reluctantly refused one as a gift.

はし HASHI Bridge

Besides the meaning expressed above, HASHI also means, "chop-sticks" and "side." Be prepared to see many more such same meaning words with different meanings placed in this book just for you.

208 Combined Kana Sound Changes Basic Kana (にゃ-Nya) To (にょ-Nyo) Stroke Order

Neko ga nyā-nyā naite iru.
The cat is meowing.

Nyūmon shita.
I started training.

Yūbin furikae kōza ni nyūkin suru ni wa dōshitara yoi no desuka?
How do I deposit funds into a postal tranfer account?

Nyuru-nyuru to tako ga ugoiteru.
An. octopus is moving.

Nyōbō wa namakemono.
My wife is lazy.

Hebi ga nyoro-nyoro to kocchi e kita.
A snake is wriggling towards this way.

Takenoko ga nyoki-nyoki to haete iru.
Young bamboo shoots are sprouting.

SIX STROKES

Today's Target Kana For Stroke Practice

Last Kana	にゃ	ニャ	Next Kana
ちょ	Hiragana Soft Cursive Writing	Katakana Stiff Square Strokes	にゅ
CHO			NYU

Hints For Stroke Order Reproduction And Recognition

(にゃ-**nya**), the pronunciation of this kana, is similar in sound to "knee ya" when pronounced quickly. For the best stroke writing results, use a felt tip pen. Start from the left and follow the arrows. Using the very first kana as an example, slowly, with a light steady hand, try to accurately form your target kana. Use all the blank box spaces and imitate the strokes of your present and last kana until your kana resemble the original ones.

Target Strokes	1	2	3	4	5	6	7	8	9
にゃ									
ニャ									

Basic Kana (にゃ-Nya) To (にょ-Nyo) Stroke Order

FOUR STROKES

Today's Target Kana For Stroke Practice

Last Kana	Hiragana Soft Cursive Writing	Katakana Stiff Square Strokes	Next Kana
にゃ	にゅ	ニュ	にょ
NYA			NYO

Hints For Stroke Order Reproduction And Recognition

(にゅ-**nyu**), the pronunciation of this kana, is similar to "knee you" when pronounced very rapidly. For the best stroke writing results, use a felt tip pen. Start from the left and follow the arrows. Using the very first kana as an example, slowly, with a light steady hand, try to accurately form your target kana. Use all the blank box spaces and imitate the strokes of your present and last kana until your kana resemble the original ones.

FIVE STROKES

Today's Target Kana For Stroke Practice

Last Kana	Hiragana Soft Cursive Writing	Katakana Stiff Square Strokes	Next Kana
にゅ	にょ	ニョ	ひゃ
NYU			HYA

Hints For Stroke Order Reproduction And Recognition

(にょ-**nyo**), the pronunciation of this kana, is similar in sound to the word "knee yo" when spoken rapidly. For the best stroke writing results use a felt tip pen. Start from the left and follow the arrows. Using the first kana as an example, slowly, with a light steady hand, try to accurately form your very first kana. Use all the blank box spaces and imitate the strokes of your present and last kana until your kana resemble the original ones.

Target Strokes	1	2	3	4	5	6	7	8	9
にょ									
ニョ									

CREATIVE KANA REVIEW

Write it! Read it! Say it!

にゃ		にゅ		にょ
NYA		NYU		NYO

LINK-A-LETTER: You have already practiced writing all the hiragana on this page. Now use them to build new words in the adjoining boxes. Then try to link them to phrases.

にゃお **nyao** a cat's meow				にゅういん **nyūin** a hospital patient			
にょうぼう **nyōbo** one's wife				にょらい **nyorai** Buddha			
にょう **nyō** urine				にゅうでん **nyūden** receive a telegram			
にゅうし **nyūshi** entrance examination				にゅうもん **nyūmon** a person's student			
にょじつ **nyojitsu** realistically				にゅうわ **nyūwa** meekness			

Identify An Object Through Hiragana

THIS ILLUSTRATION CONTAINS 12 OBJECTS WHICH WHEN TRANSLATED FROM THEIR CLUE HIRAGANA WORDS INTO ROMANIZED JAPANESE ALL BEGIN WITH THE LETTER 'T.' SEE HOW QUICKLY YOU CAN MATCH THE CORRECT OBJECT WITH ITS HIRAGANA WORD.

1	つ り	4	てんと	7	とんぼ	10	た け
2	たばこ	5	とけい	8	てっぽう	11	つ ぼ
3	たきび	6	たいや	9	たんぽぽ	12	とまと

Vocabulary Expanding For Interacting

Making Comparisons

NATURAL SURVIVAL CONVERSATION

What You Might Hear	How You Might Possibly Answer
(O) **Kare no taido wa mae yori motto yoku natta.** (E) His manners are better than before.	(P) **Jikan-dōri kare ga kuru kara desu ka?** (E) Do you say that because he's on time?
(O) **Nihonjin wa hoka no ajia-jin yori eigo ga motto heta desu ka?** (E) Are Japanese poorer at English than other Asians?	(C) **Nihonjin yori hoka no ajia-jin no hō ga eigo o jōzu ni shaberu yō da.** (E) It seems that other Asians speak better English than Japanese people.
(O) **Kawatta kuruma o doko de kau ka chie o shibotte iru.** (E) I'm racking my brains thinking where to buy an unusual car.	(O) **Kono kon-iro no kuruma wa ano kuruma yori atarashii desu.** (E) This navy blue colored car is newer than that car.
(P) **Kore wa dō desu ka?** (E) How do you like this one?	(P) **Ano hō ga yasuin desu.** (E) That one's cheaper.
(O) **Watashi no furusato wa Tokyo yori sumigokochi ga ii.** (E) It's more comfortable to live in my hometown than in Tokyo.	(C) **Tokyo wa sekai de ichiban bukka ga takai machida kara ne.** (E) That's because Tokyo is the most expensive city in the world.
(O) **Fuji-san wa nihon de mottomo nadakai yama desu.** (E) Mt. Fuji is the most famous mountain in Japan.	(O) **Keredomo kenia no kirimanjaro wa motto kirei desu.** (E) But Mt. Kilimanjaro of Kenya is prettier.
(O) **Ame ga furu ka na!** (E) I wonder if it'll rain.	(O) **Kyonen no tenki to kuraberu to kotoshi wa ame ga ōi.** (E) In comparison with last year's weather, we have had more rain this year.
(O) **Ima hajimeru no to kinyōbi made matsu no to dō chigaimasu ka?** (E) What's the difference between waiting until Friday and starting now?	(O) **Motto hiyō o herasere ba soredake ii kara.** (E) Because the sooner we plan to cut costs the better.

NATURAL SURVIVAL CONVERSATION

What You Might Hear	How You Might Possibly Answer
(O) **Iro-iro na koto suru no ni boku no hō ga anata yori motto kichin to dekiru.** (E) I am more organized at doing things than you.	(O) **Kare wa kuchi dake de jissai wa nani mo shite-kure-nai.** (E) He gives lip service but not a helping hand.
(P) **Kare no keiei nōryoku o dō omoimasu ka ?** (E) How do you feel about his business management ability ?	(O) **Kare wa ichiban ōi yosan kara ichiban sukunai yosan ni herashita.** (E) He lowered the budget from one of the highest to one of the lowest.

DOODLE Fun With Hiragana Combinations

ごんべのななし

The person called Gombei has no name

へのへのもへじ

(words of no real meaning)

フルかわ

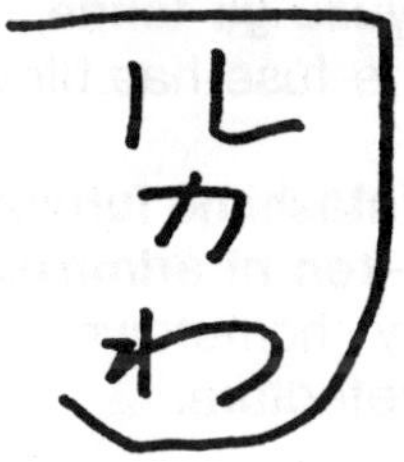

Furukawa, a common family name

なかむらかつひこ

I'm Katsuhiko Nakamura

ちちのはみがく

Brush your father's teeth

ままのへそ

Mother's navel cord

216 Combined Kana Sound Changes
Basic Kana (ひゃ-Hya) To (ひょ-Hyo) Stroke Order

Hyakuman desu.
It's one million.

Watashi wa metta ni hyākkaten de kaimono wa shinai.
I seldom shop in department stores.

Tokyo ni aru Hyakkaen o bura-bura shimashō.
Let's stroll in Tokyo's 100 Flowers Park.

Hyūzu ga tonda.
The fuse has blown out.

Watashi no furusato no Hyūga wa Miyazaki-ken ni arimasu.
My hometown, Hyūga, is in Miyazaki Prefecture.

Kare wa hyōban ga warui.
He has a bad reputation.

Kono keikoku o hyōshiki ni kaite kudasai.
Please put this notice on the bulletin board.

Dō shimashita ka? Ukanai hyōjō desu ne.
What's wrong? You look pretty gloomy.

FOUR STROKES

Today's Target Kana For Stroke Practice

Last Kana	Hiragana Soft Cursive Writing	Katakana Stiff Square Strokes	Next Kana
にょ	ひゃ	ヒャ	ひゅ
NYO			HYU

Hints For Stroke Order Reproduction And Recognition

(ひゃ-**hya**), the pronunciation of this kana, is similar to the sound of the 'home-made' word "he-yah" when pronounced very quickly. For the best stroke writing results use a felt tip pen. Always start from the left and follow the arrows. Using the first kana as an example, slowly, with a light steady hand, try to accurately form your very first kana. Use all the blank box spaces and repeat until your kana resemble the original ones.

Target Strokes	1	2	3	4	5	6	7	8	9
ひゃ	ひ	ひっ	ひゃ	ひゃ					
ヒャ	ノ	ヒ	ヒっ	ヒャ					

TWO STROKES

Today's Target Kana For Stroke Practice

Last Kana	Hiragana Soft Cursive Writing	Katakana Stiff Square Strokes	Next Kana
ひゃ	ひゅ	ヒュ	ひょ
HYA			HYO

Hints For Stroke Order Reproduction And Recognition

(ひゅ-**hyu**), the pronunciation of this kana, is similar to the sound of these two joined pronouns "he-you", when pronounced very quickly. For the best stroke writing results use a felt tip pen. Start from the left and follow the arrows. Using the first kana as an example, slowly, with a light steady hand, try to accurately form your very first kana. Use all the blank box spaces and repeat until your kana resemble the original ones.

Target Strokes	1	2	3	4	5	6	7	8	9
ひゅ	ひ	ひゅ							
ヒュ	ノ	ヒ	ヒ	ヒュ					

THREE STROKES

Today's Target Kana For Stroke Practice

Last Kana	Hiragana	Katakana	Next Kana
ひゅ	ひょ	ヒョ	みゃ
HYU	Hiragana Soft Cursive Writing	Katakana Stiff Square Strokes	MYA

Hints For Stroke Order Reproduction And Recognition

(ひょ-**hyo**) the pronunciation of this kana, is similar to the sound of the pronoun "he" and the word "yo" when spoken rapidly. For the best stroke writing results use a felt tip pen. Always start from the left and follow the arrows. Using the first kana as an example, slowly, with a light steady hand, try to accurately form your very first kana. Use all the blank box spaces and repeat until your kana resemble the original ones.

Target Strokes	1	2	3	4	5	6	7	8	9
ひょ	ひ	ひ	ひょ						
ヒョ	ノ	ヒ	ヒ	ヒョ	ヒョ				

Basic Kana (ひゃ-Hya) To (ひょ-Hyo) Stroke Order

CREATIVE KANA REVIEW

Write it! Read it! Say it!

ひゃ		ひゅ		ひょ
HYA		HYU		HYO

LINK-A-LETTER: You have already practiced writing all the hiragana on this page. Now use them to build new words in the adjoining boxes. Then try to link them to phrases.

ひゃく **hyaku** one hundred		ひょうさつ **hyōsatsu** a sign board
ひゃくまん **hyakuman** one million		ひょう **hyō** iceberg
ひょうし **hyōshi** book cover		ひゃくやく **hyakuyaku** best of all
ひょうしき **hyōshiki** traffic sign		ひゅう **hyū** to hiss (or) whistle
ひょうしょう **hyōshō** to award a prize		ひょいと **hyoito** unexpectedly

HERE'S A SIMPLE WAY TO LEARN LETTERS AND WORDS CREATIVELY WHILE SAMPLING SOME OF JAPAN'S CULTURE. HIRAGANA IDEOGRAMS ARE MISSING IN THE BOXES ABOVE THE ROMANIZED VERSION OF THEIR SOUNDS TO COMPLETE A WORD, MERELY DIG INTO THE LETTER BOX CONTAINING ALL THE LETTERS NEEDED. AFTER THAT, WITH THE POSSIBLE HELP OF A JAPANESE ACQUAINTANCE OR A ROMANIZED DICTIONARY, GROUP ALL THE WORDS INTO A SENTENCE.

Example:
HOT BARLEY TEA (**MUGI-CHA**) TASTES GOOD IN THE WINTERTIME. (ぎ) IS THE MISSING LETTER FOR BOX NUMBER TWO. WRITE IT IN.

1	2	3
む		ちゃ
MU	**GI**	**CHA**

Now you can dig into the letter box for letters to fill in the boxes below.

Quizzeria

1) Makes a delightful sound when the wind blows

ふう		
FU	**RI**	**N**

2) A small cup used to drink rice wine.

さ	か		
SA	**KA**	**ZU**	**KI**

3) A traditional Japanese style inn.

り			ん
	RYO	**KA**	**N**

222 Sets Of Ko(こ)-So(そ)-A(あ)-Do(ど) Words

There are three special groups of words for the "this" and "that" which are better known as **ko-so-a-do (doko)** words. They are namely **kore**, **sore**, and **are**. The demonstrative words **kono**, **sono**, and **ano** are used with nouns and have a similar purpose as the **ko-so-a-do** words. That is to indicate something from the viewpoint of the speaker uttering those words.

	Near the speaker	Near the listener	Remote from both the speaker and the listener	
BASE	**ko** words	**so** words	**a** words	**do** words
direction	**kochira** here, this way	**sochira** there, that way	**achira** over there	**dochira** where
people	**kochira** this person	**sochira** that person	**achira** that person over there	**donata** **dare** who
thing	**kore** this	**sore** that	**are** that over there	**dore** which
place	**koko** here	**soko** there	**asoko** over there	**doko** where
demonstrative	**kono** this **korera** these	**sono** that **sorera** those	**ano** that over there **arera** those	**dono** which

Examples :

(O) **Kono seki o mihatte ite kudasai.**
(E) Please keep this seat for me.

(O) **Sonna ni busahō ni shinai de.**
(E) Don't be that rude.

(O) **Shakkuri no yoi naoshikata wa nan desu ka ?**
(E) What's a good cure for hiccups ?

(O) **Karera wa michi o noro-noro aruite iru.**
(E) They are walking slowly on the street.

Interrogative words		
Who	**Which**	**What**
dare **dare no**	**dochira** (of two) **dore** (of any number) **dochira no** (of two) **dono** (of any number)	**nani** **nani, nan no, dō iu**

Examples :	**dōshite**	**naze**	**itsu**	**dō**	**ikaga**
	how (or) why	why	when	how	how about

(O) **Itsu okiru no desu ka ?**
(E) When do you get up ?

(O) **Ocha wa ikaga desu ka ?**
(E) How about a cup of tea ?

(O) **Naze kono akishitsu wa sōji sarete inai desu ka ?**
(E) Why hasn't this vacant room been cleaned ?

Adverbs Of Cause, Manner and Degree

naze	**dono yō ni**	**kono yō ni**	**taihen**	**kiwamete**
why	how	so (or) thus	very	quite

tada	**daibubun**	**gurai**	**dō yō ni**
only (or) free	almost	approximately	similarly

224 Sets Of Ko(こ)-So(そ)-A(あ)-Do(ど) Words

Adverbs of Time

itsumo	**taigai**	**shiba-shiba**	**tokidoki**	**mata**
always	usually	often	sometimes	again
itsu	**sono toki**	**ima**	**saikin**	**mamonaku**
when	then	now	recently	soon
sugu	**ato de**	**izen**	**saigo ni**	
directly	later	formerly	finally	

Tense Indicators

Present Tense

The present tense of a word will always end with **u** sound. Verbs which do not end with the simple **u** will end with either **eru**, **iru**, **e**, **i**, **ere**, or **ire**. The four important irregular verbs are **aru** (to be), **kuru** (to come), **suru** (to do) and **masu** (a verbal suffix for honorific conjugation). Thus words and phrases or sentences will end in the present as shown.

U Example : **tayoru** (or) **makaseru**
to depend on — leave it up to you

Su Example : **masu**
to do, perform, or accomplish

Arimasu Example : **takusan gomi ga arimasu**
there is a lot of trash

Polite form of **aru** meaning 'exists' or 'there is.' '**Desu**', is a copula in the polite form meaning 'there is.'

(P) **Amari imi o nasanai desu.**
(E) You're not making much sense.

(P) **Fukai ni shitara warui desu.**
(E) It's bad to cause inconvenience to others.

Past Tense

The past tense is formed by adding ta to the end of a verb, words, phrases, or sentences ending in the past tense as in the following.

Ta Example : **Nihongo de tegami o kaita.**
I wrote a letter in Japanese.

Deshita Example : **Nagai koto ome ni kakarimasen deshita.**
(past tense of '**desu**') I haven't seen you for a long time.

Shita Example : **Kimi no kao o omoidashimashita.**
I thought about you.
(said to intimate friends only)

Simple and Probable Future Tense

The future tense can be made either by using the simple u or the probable form which is done by the selection of either of these two particles—**deshō** or **darō**. Look at these examples of future actions.

Iku Example : **Raishū furansu e iku.**
I'll go to France next week.

Darō Example : **Hayaku netara ii darō.**
It's probably alright to sleep early.

Deshō Example : **Asu Ibe-san ga kuru deshō.**
Mr. Ibe probably will come tomorrow.

Affirmative Future tense

Sho
'may', 'perhaps', 'will be', or 'probably'
Example : (P) **Sugano-san demo sasoimasho !**
(E) Let's ask Mr. Sugano !

Masho
'let's or 'let's do it'

Any sentences ending with **'masho'** or **'desho'** are indications of the future tense.

Summary

A verb is any word which ends with **masu**, and as a rule all verbs end with **masu.** To make a word a past tense merely switch the ending from **masu** to **mashita. Mashita** refers to a past action. We form a past negative by using the two words **masen deshita.**

Masu, masen, mashita, and **masen deshita** are all verbs. A non-past tense or indicator can describe the present or the future with **masu**.

Onomatopoetic Words Found In This Book

A distinctive feature of the Japanese language is its rich variety of fun word-sound combinations called onomatopoeia, which people often use in conversation to express not only human feelings but also to describe action sounds and states of being in daily life styles. Such sound symbolisms are important as they are a vital part of adult spoken and written Japanese. As some matters cannot be expressed without the use of onomatopoeia, such sounds are very effective when used correctly and skillfully. Thus you'll come across them in various chapters of this book. For recognition purposes notice these underlined samples.

(O) **Kodomo wa** sono **inu ni** <u>**odo-odo**</u> **shita**.
(E) The child was <u>frightened</u> by that dog.

(O) **Onna wa** <u>**kera-kera**</u> **warau, otoko wa** <u>**kusu-kusu**</u> **warau**.
(E) A woman <u>cackles</u> and a man chuckles.

(O) **Obuchi-san wa** <u>**zun-zun**</u> **aruita**.
(E) Mr. Obuchi walked <u>swiftly</u> with a strong forceful stride.

(P) <u>**Doshi-doshi**</u> **tegami o kudasai.**
(E) Please write to me <u>constantly</u>.

A Winter Happening In Japan Quiz 227

THESE ARE ARTICLES INDIGENOUS TO A JAPANESE NEW YEARS CELEBRATION. COMPLETE EACH WORD BY USING A ROMANIZED JAPANESE DICTIONARY AND THEN WRITE THEIR HIRAGANA VERSION FOR WRITING PRACTICE.

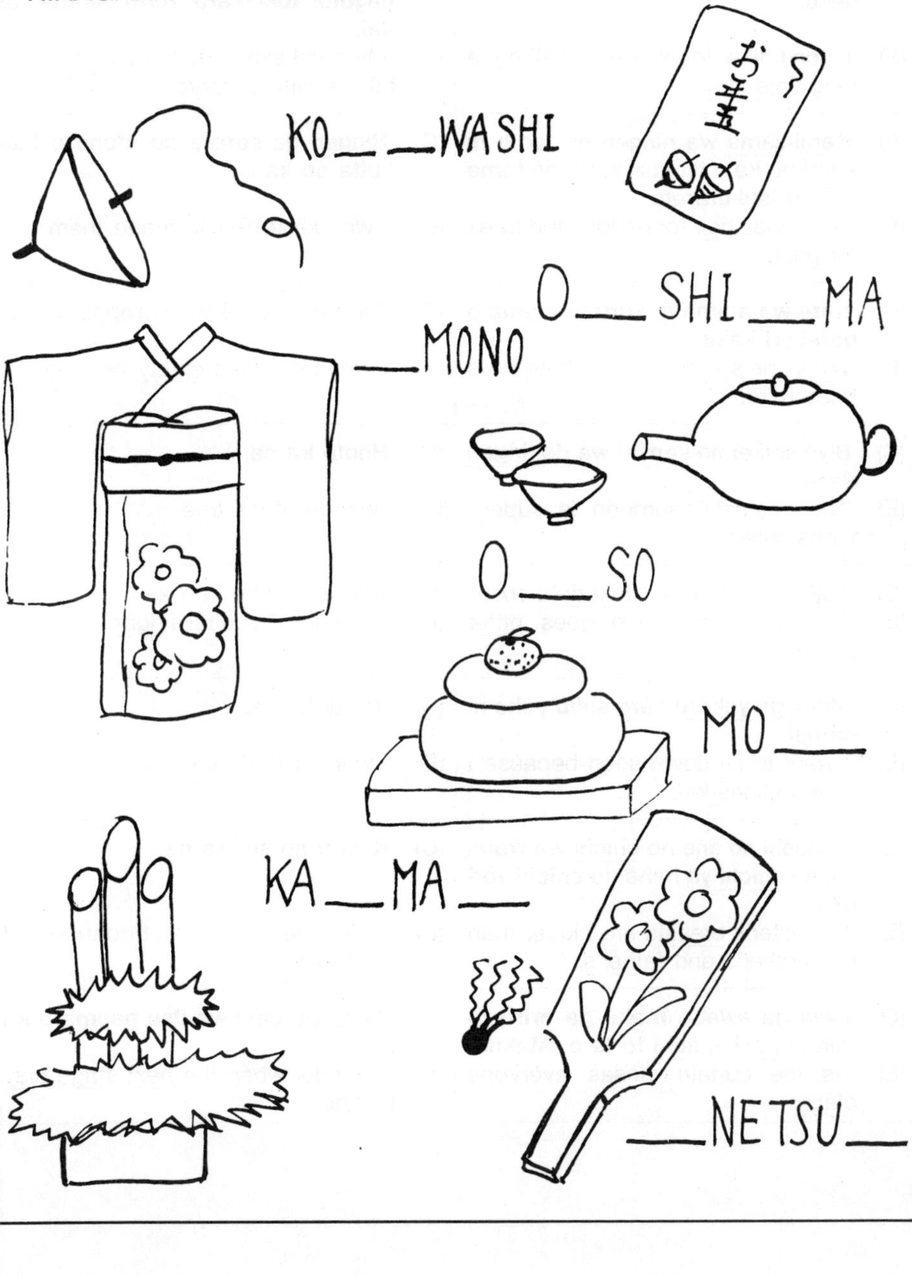

228

Vocabulary Expanding For Interacting Using 'Ka Na' And The Human Anatomy Limbs

NATURAL SURVIVAL CONVERSATION

What You Might Hear	How You Might Possibly Answer
(O) **Nagaku matasareru no wa iya desu.** (E) I don't like to be kept waiting a long time.	(O) **Kare ga ita de watashi no atama o nagutta toki kara zutto atama ga itai.** (E) My head still hurts from the time he hit me with a board.
(P) **Kami-sama wa ningen no tame ni kami no ke o tsukuri kami no tame ni ki o tsukurareta.** (E) God made hair for people and trees for paper.	(C) **Ningen ga sorera no mono o tsukutta no ka na.** (E) I wonder if people made them.
(C) **Kare wa atama ni kuru to atama o bori-bori kaku.** (E) When he's mad he scratches his head hard.	(C) **Kare no atama wa karappo ka na.** (E) I wonder if he's empty headed.
(C) **Biyō seikei no sensei wa dokingan desu.** (E) The cosmetic surgeon is super-shortsighted.	(C) **Honto ka na.** (E) I wonder if it's true.
(C) **Tokidoki mune ga doki-doki suru.** (E) Sometimes my heart goes pitter patter.	(C) **Anata daijōbu ka na.** (E) I wonder if you're alright.
(C) **Mune ga yakeru kara sugu yoko ni naritai.** (E) I want to lie down soon because I have indigestion.	(C) **Warui ka na.** (E) I wonder if it's bad.
(O) **Watashi no ane no chichi wa watashi no chichi ya haha no chichi yori ōkii.** (E) My sister's breasts are bigger than my mother's and father's.	(C) **Kusuri no sei ka na.** (E) I wonder if it's because of medicine.
(O) **Geki ga owatte maku ga oriru to minna pachi-pachi to te o tataku.** (E) As the curtain closes everyone claps.	(C) **Tsugi no geki wa itsu hajimaru ka na.** (E) I wonder when the next stage play begins.

229

Vocabulary Expanding For Interacting Using 'Ka Na' And The Human Anatomy Limbs

NATURAL SURVIVAL CONVERSATION

What You Might Hear	How You Might Possibly Answer
(O) **Kurubushi o itameta.** (E) I hurt my ankle.	(C) **Aruku no wa mendō dewa nai no ka na.** (E) I wonder if it's troublesome to walk.
(O) **Kanojo no ashi wa buyo-buyo shite iru kara miryoku ga nai.** (E) Her legs are very flabby and unappealing.	(C) **Dōshite ka na.** (E) I wonder why.
(C) **Kare wa ofuro ni haitte nakkatta ka na.** (E) I wonder if he took a bath.	(O) **Kare no aka darake no hifu ga aka cha-iro da.** (E) His dirty skin is reddish brown.
(O) **Ano yowaimono-ijime o suru yatsu ga kerarete taoreta.** (E) That bully got kicked and fell.	(C) **Dare ga kettaka wakatta ka na.** (E) I wonder if he saw who kicked him.

DOODLE Fun With Hiragana Combinations

そこそこきけん

Caution! It's a dangerous place

もりもりくえよ

Eat up!

ハマムラ

Hamamura—a family name

230 Combined Kana Sound Changes
Basic Kana (みゃ-Mya) To (みょ-Myo) Stroke Order

Checking the pulse

Myaku o hakaru.
Taking the pulse.

Kare no hanashi niwa myakuraku ga nai.
There's no line of reasoning in what he says.

Onsen ga myaku-myaku to waite iru.
Hot spring water is gushing out.

Watashi wa myukenai bunka o shiranai.
I don't understand the Mycenae culture.

Myunhen wa biiru de yūmei desu.
Munich is famous for its beer.

Watashi wa myūjikaru ga suki da.
I like musicals.

A musical

Family name

Myōgonichi tori ni ikimasu.
I'll come to get it the day after tomorrow.

Myōchō aimashō.
Let's meet tomorrow morning.

Kare wa myō na yatsu da.
He's a rather peculiar guy.

Myōban oide kudasai.
Please come tomorrow evening.

FIVE STROKES

Today's Target Kana For Stroke Practice

Last Kana	Hiragana Soft Cursive Writing	Katakana Stiff Square Strokes	Next Kana
ひょ	みゃ	ミャ	みゅ
HYO			MYU

Hints For Stroke Order Reproduction And Recognition

(みゃ-**mya**), the pronunciation of this kana, is similar in sound to the pronoun "me" added to the word "ya" and spoken very quickly. For the best stroke writing results, use a felt tip pen. Start from the left and follow the arrows. Using the very first kana as an example, slowly, with a light steady hand, try to accurately form your target kana. Use all the blank box spaces and imitate the strokes of your present and last kana until your kana resemble the original ones.

Target Strokes	1	2	3	4	5	6	7	8	9
みゃ									
ミャ									

Basic Kana (みゃ-Mya) To (みょ-Myo) Stroke Order

THREE STROKES

Today's Target Kana For Stroke Practice

Last Kana	Hiragana Soft Cursive Writing	Katakana Stiff Square Strokes	Next Kana
みゃ	みゅ	ミュ	みょ
MYA			MYO

Hints For Stroke Order Reproduction And Recognition

(みゅ-**myu**), the pronunciation of this kana, is similar to the first syllable of the word "music". For the best stroke writing results, use a felt tip pen. Start from the left and follow the arrows. Using the very first kana as an example, slowly, with a light steady hand, try to accurately form your target kana. Use all the blank box spaces and imitate the strokes of your present and last kana until your kana resemble the original ones.

Target Strokes	1	2	3	4	5	6	7	8	9
みゅ	み	み	みゅ						
ミュ	ヽ	ミ	ミ	ミ	ミュ				

FOUR STROKES

Today's Target Kana For Stroke Practice

Last Kana: みゅ MYU

みょ ミョ

Hiragana Soft Cursive Writing

Katakana Stiff Square Strokes

Next Kana: りゃ RYA

Hints For Stroke Order Reproduction And Recognition

(みょ-**myo**), the pronunciation of this kana, is similar to the sound of the pronoun "me" plus "yo" when spoken very quickly. For the best stroke writing results, use a felt tip pen. Start from the left and follow the arrows. Using the very first kana as an example, slowly, with a light steady hand, try to accurately form your target kana. Use all the blank box spaces and imitate the strokes of your present and last kana until your kana resemble the original ones.

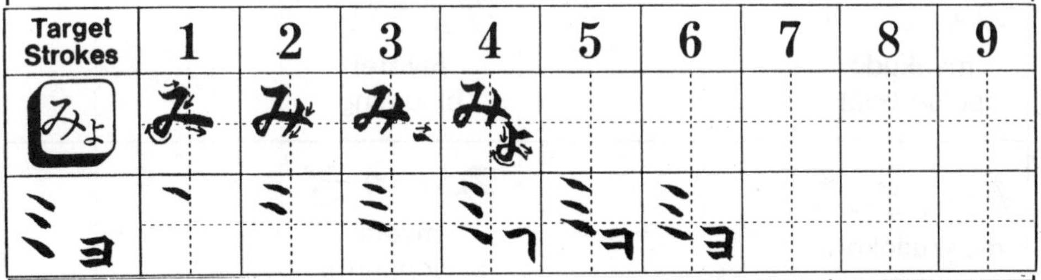

CREATIVE KANA REVIEW

Write it! Read it! Say it!

みゃ		みゅ		みょ
MYA		MYU		MYO

LINK-A-LETTER: You have already practiced writing all the hiragana on this page. Now use them to build new words in the adjoining boxes. Then try to link them to phrases.

みゃくはく **myakuhaku** heartbeat				みょうじ **myōji** family name		
みゃくどう **myakudō** pulse beat				みょうれい **myōrei** blooming		
みゃくどころ **myakudokoro** wrist				みょうぎ **myōgi** a wonderful performance		
みょうやく **myōyaku** remedy				みょうしゅ **myōshu** excellent skill		
みょうにち **myōnichi** tomorrow				みゅうじっく **myūzikku** a music		

Give ひらがな Translation A Try

The above basic movements are fairly obvious. Try your hand at translating all 16 actions into Romaji and then English with the aid of a Japanese acquaintance or a Romanized Japanese dictionary. Then try to make short sentences with them in Romaji and hiragana. Good luck! **(Ganbatte!)**

1.うつ　2.とまる　3.あがる/のぼる　4.さがる/くだる

5.とぶ　6.とぶ　7.すべる　8.ころがる

9.たつ　10.たおれる　11.まがる　12.おれる

13.はいる　14.でる　15.おちる　16.まわる

236 Translating Basic Human Reflective Actions

TEST YOURSELF ON HOW QUICKLY AND ACCURATELY YOU CAN TRANSLATE THESE ACTIONS INTO ENGLISH. HAVE A JAPANESE CHECK THEM IF POSSIBLE AND THEN PRACTICE WRITING ALL OF THEM IN HIRAGANA FOR VOCABULARY BUILDING.

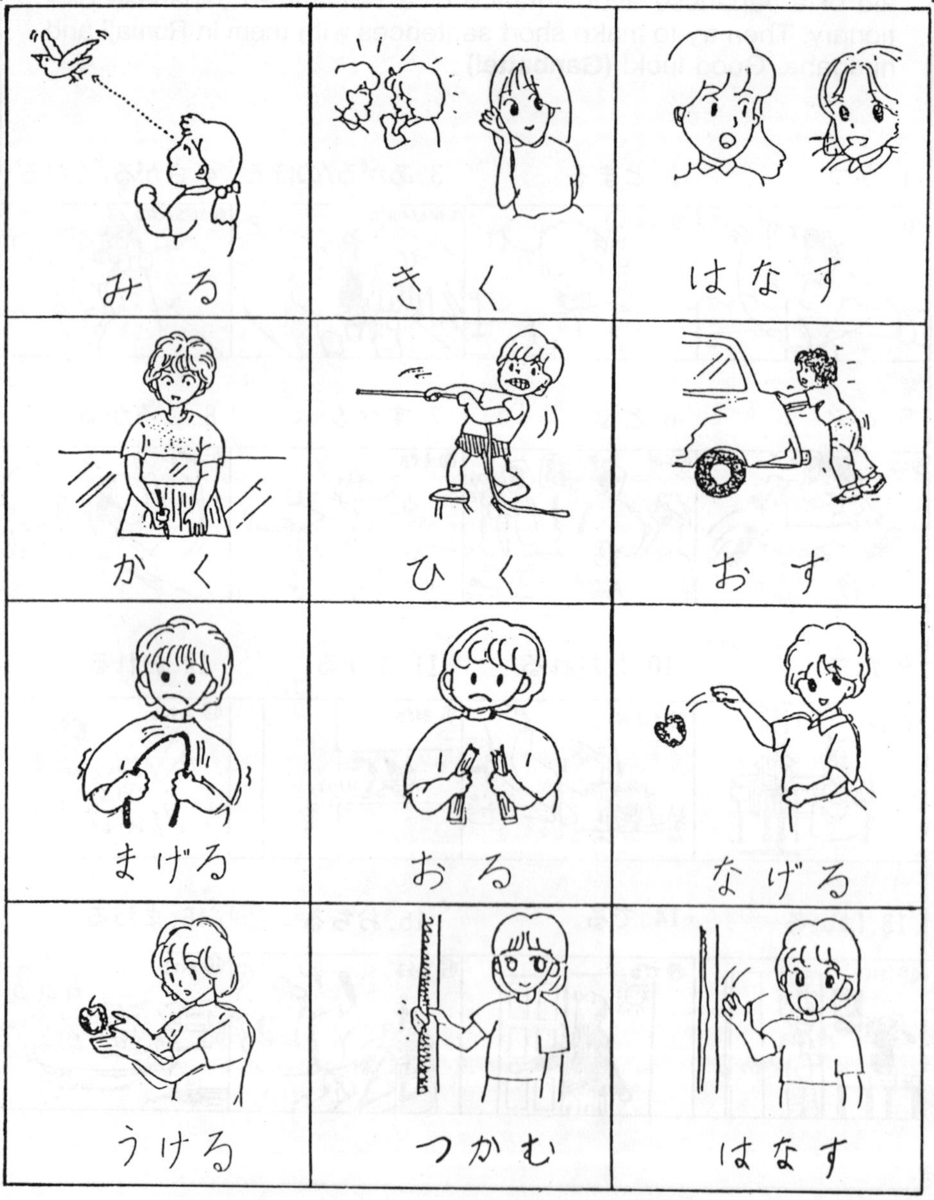

Basic Human Reflective Moods Writing Practice 237

A ROMANIZED JAPANESE DICTIONARY OR JAPANESE PERSON CAN BE HELPFUL IN KNOWING THESE ILLUSTRATED MOODS. PRACTICE WRITING THEM IN HIRAGANA FOR ACCURACY AND VOCABULARY BUILDING.

わらっている

かんがえている

ないている

つかれている

はなしている

しんぱいしている

ねむっている

おこる

うれしい

Vocabulary Expanding For Interacting

Trying To Make Friends

NATURAL SURVIVAL CONVERSATION

What You Might Hear	How You Might Possibly Answer
(C) **Yā Genki.** (E) Hi! How are you?	(O) **Genki desu. Yoi kayōbi de arimasu yō ni.** (E) Just fine. Happy Tuesday to you.
(P) **Soto wa tottemo suteki desu.** (E) It's pretty nice out.	(P) **Doko ka de o ai shimasen deshita ka?** (E) Haven't we met somewhere before?
(O) **Iie sō wa omoimasen.** (E) No, I don't think so.	(O) **Sore wa senshū no getsuyōbi no gogo toshokan deshita.** (E) It was in the library last Monday afternoon.
(O) **Kioku ryoku ga yoi desu ne.** (E) You have a good memory.	(O) **Soshite anata wa shiranu-ma ni kieta.** (E) And then you disappeared like rain into the soil.
(O) **Barabō ojisan to au yakusoku o shimashita.** (E) I had an appointment with my Uncle Baraboo.	(P) **Mata o-ai dekite ureshii desu.** (E) It's nice to see you again.
(O) **Ome ni kakarete ureshii desu.** (E) It's nice to be seen.	(O) **Watashi ni totte suteki na yoru desu.** (E) It's a lovely evening for me.
(P) **Itsuka goissho ni ikaga desu ka?** (E) Would you care to spend some time with me?	(O) **Honki desu ka soretomo iikagen na koto o yutte irun desu ka?** (E) Are you serious or delirious?
(O) **Hataraite inai toki, isogashiku nai toki, biyō no tame inemuri o shite inai toki, tanoshimi ni nani o shimasu ka?** (E) What do you do for fun when you're not (working? / busy? / beauty-napping?)	(O) **Watashi wa ichinichi sei ippai ikiru ningen no yoi tehon desu.** (E) I'm a good example of someone who lives one day at a time.

NATURAL SURVIVAL CONVERSATION

What You Might Hear	How You Might Possibly Answer
(C) **<u>Sekenzure</u> shite iru?** (E) Are you street-wise?	(O) **Deito niwa ososugiru shi tomodachi ni naru niwa hayasugiru.** (E) It's too late for dating and too early for friendship.
(O) **Yaru koto wa subete yatta.** (E) You can't say I didn't try.	(C) **Nante itta no?** (W) What did you say?
(C) **Hitori goto sa.** (M) I was just talking to myself.	(O) **Komban wa kore de owari ni shiyō!** (E) Let's call it an evening.
(O) **Aete ureshi katta.** (E) It was good to see you.	(O) **Onaji yō ni.** (E) Like-wise.

DOODLE Fun With Hiragana Combinations

しめんそか

Many enemies around me

へのへのじしん

Pay attention to earthquakes

のうてんキ

The optimist

240 Combined Kana Sound Changes
Basic Kana (りゃ-Rya) To (りょ-Ryo) Stroke Order

Nan no ryakuji desu ka?
What fully spelt logogram does this simplified version stand for?

Ryakushiki de kekkonshiki o ageru.
I'll have a very informal wedding ceremony.

Kūki no ryūtsū ga nai.
There's no ventilation in here.

Kare wa kane o seiji mokuteki de ryūyō shimashita.
He diverted some money for political purposes.

Kare wa kinniku ryūryū da.
His muscles are bulging.

Karera wa tagai ni ryōkai shita.
They reached a mutual understanding.

Furusato e ryōyō ni iku.
I'm making a trip to my hometown.

Kin niman-en ryōshū shimashita.
I acknowledge receipt of the amount of 20,000 yen.

FIVE STROKES

Today's Target Kana For Stroke Practice

Last Kana	Hiragana Soft Cursive Writing	Katakana Stiff Square Strokes	Next Kana
みょ	りゃ	リャ	りゅ
MYO			RYU

Hints For Stroke Order Reproduction And Recognition

(りゃ-**rya**), the pronunciation of this kana, is similar in sound to the Korean name "Rhee" plus "ya" when spoken very quickly. For the best stroke writing results, use a felt tip pen. Start from the left and follow the arrows. Using the very first kana as an example, slowly, with a light steady hand, try to accurately form your target kana. Use all the blank box spaces and imitate the strokes of your present and last kana until your kana resemble the original ones.

Target Strokes	1	2	3	4	5	6	7	8	9
りゃ									
リャ									

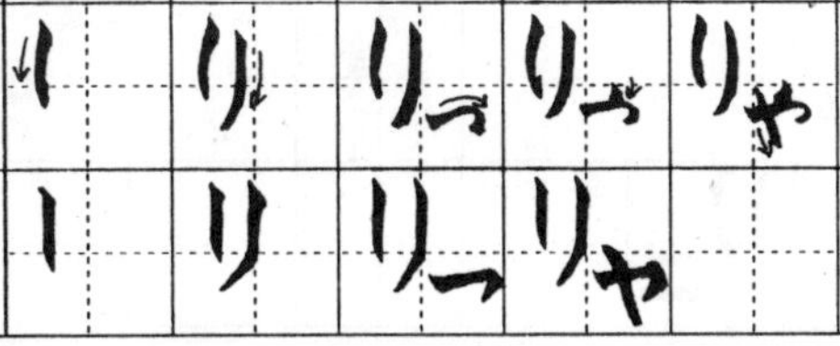

THREE STROKES

Today's Target Kana For Stroke Practice

Last Kana	Hiragana Soft Cursive Writing	Katakana Stiff Square Strokes	Next Kana
りゃ	りゅ	リュ	りょ
RYA			RYO

Hints For Stroke Order Reproduction And Recognition

(りゅ-**ryu**), the pronunciation of this kana, is similar in sound to the Korean name "Rhee" with the added pronoun "you" when spoken very quickly. For the best stroke writing results, use a felt tip pen. Start from the left and follow the arrows. Using the very first kana as an example, slowly, with a light steady hand, try to accurately form your target kana. Use all the blank box spaces and imitate the strokes of your present and last kana until your kana resemble the original ones.

Target Strokes	1	2	3	4	5	6	7	8	9
りゅ		り	りゅ						
リュ		リ		リュ					

FOUR STROKES

Today's Target Kana For Stroke Practice

Last Kana	Hiragana Soft Cursive Writing	Katakana Stiff Square Strokes	Next Kana
りゅ	りょ	リョ	ぎゃ
RYU			GYA

Hints For Stroke Order Reproduction And Recognition

(りょ-**ryo**), the pronunciation of this kana, is similar in sound to the Latin American city "Rio". For the best stroke writing results, use a felt tip pen. Start from the left and follow the arrows. Using the very first kana as an example, slowly, with a light steady hand, try to accurately form your target kana. Use all the blank box spaces and imitate the strokes of your present and last kana until your kana resemble the original ones.

Target Strokes	1	2	3	4	5	6	7	8	9
りょ		り	り	りょ					
リョ		リ	リ	リョ					

Basic Kana (りゃ-Rya) To (りょ-Ryo) Stroke Order

CREATIVE KANA REVIEW

Write it! Read it! Say it!

りゃ		りゅ		りょ
RYA		RYU		RYO

LINK-A-LETTER: You have already practiced writing all the hiragana on this page. Now use them to build new words in the adjoining boxes. Then try to link them to phrases.

りょかん **ryokan** a Japanese inn				りゅう **ryū** dragon			
りゃくず **ryakuzu** a sketch				りょうり **ryōri** to cook			
りゅうがく **ryūgaku** to study abroad				りょうしん **ryōshin** parents			
りょこう **ryokō** to travel				りょうほう **ryōhō** both			
りょうじかん **ryōjikan** consulate				りゅうこう **ryūkō** fashion			

Make A Hiragana Word 245

VOCABULARY BUILDER

RANDOMLY PICK CIRCLED LETTERS NEXT TO AN OBJECT. THEN ADD ENOUGH HIRAGANA IDEOGRAMS TO FORM A COMPLETE WORD. A ROMANIZED JAPANESE DICTIONARY CAN AID IN MAKING TWELVE WORDS TO PUT NEXT TO THE NUMBERS BELOW. EXAMPLE : (ゆめ-DREAM).

1 ______	4 ______	7 ______	10 ______
2 ______	5 ______	8 ______	11 ______
3 ______	6 ______	9 ______	12 ______

Vocabulary Expanding For Interacting

Talking Around The Dinner Table

NATURAL SURVIVAL CONVERSATION

What You Might Hear	How You Might Possibly Answer
(O) **Komban wa. Watashi wa hashi no hashi de chūgoku no hashi o mitsu-keta.** (E) Good evening. I found a pair of Chinese chopsticks at the edge of a bridge.	(O) **Jikan-dōri tabemasu.** (E) We eat on time.
(C) **Otto kara ō-medama o kutta.** (W) I got a severe scolding from my husband.	(O) **Mata tabemono o kogashimashita ka?** (M) Did you burn the food again?
(O) **Yūshoku ni nani o tabemasu ka?** (E) What are we having for dinner?	(O) **Kinō no itan de inai nokorimono ga amatte iru.** (E) We have unspoilt food left over from yesterday.
(O) **Dokumanjū o tabete neko ga ne-konda.** (E) The cat wound up sick from poisonous sweet dumplings.	(O) **Shokuyoku ga zannen nagara na-kunarimashita.** (E) I'm afraid I've lost my appetite.
(O) **Ue no gakusei wa itsumo uete iru.** (E) The student upstairs is always hungry.	(O) **Aji no himono wa aji ga yoi.** (E) Sun-dried fish tastes good.
(O) **Obuchi-san wa hara ga hette ita no de sono tabemono o gatsu-gatsu to tabeta.** (M) As he was hungry, Mr. Obuchi wolfed down his food.	(O) **Nihonjin wa itsumo mono o taberu toki ni kucha-kucha to oto o tateru.** (E) Japanese always make noise when they eat.
(O) **Watashi wa itsumo kuchi o tojite tabemono o nomi-komimasu.** (E) I always swallow food with my mouth closed.	(O) **Oozei no hito ga anata no tabekata o manetara ii deshō.** (E) It would be nice if many people followed your eating habits.
(O) **Watashi no haha wa umai pan o yaku no ga umai.** (E) My mother is good at baking tasty bread.	(O) **Suki ni naru ka dō ka kakushin wa arimasen.** (E) I'm not convinced I'll get to like it.

NATURAL SURVIVAL CONVERSATION

What You Might Hear	How You Might Possibly Answer
(O) **Nodo ga kara-kara ni kawaita.** (E) My throat is very parched.	(O) **Biiru wa dō desu ka?** (E) How about a beer?
(O) **Mizu dake o nomu.** (E) I only drink water.	(O) **Sore ja anata no kenkō o shukufuku shite kampai.** (E) Well then, here's to your health.
(O) **Nihon-shiki no kaze no naoshi kata wa nan desu ka?** (E) What's the Japanese remedy for curing a cold?	(O) **Kaze o naoshitai nara atsui o-sake o nondara sugu naoru.** (E) If you want to get rid of your cold drinking hot rice wine will do it.
(O) **Rubio-san wa doko ni imasu ka?** (E) Where's Mr. Rubio?	(O) **Ima kare wa suki na terebi bangumi o minagara ima de tabako o sutte imasu.** (E) Right now he's in the living-room, smoking and watching his favorite tv program.

DOODLE Fun With Hiragana Combinations

ここもへき

Please come here.

へめへめりへし

Dear Mary

へのへのひけし

Prevent fires.

248 Combined Kana Sound Changes
Basic Kana (ぎゃ-Gya) To (ぎょ-Gyo) Stroke Order

Kare wa gyakujō shita.
He got really angry.

Gyūniku o tabete iru.
I'm eating beef.

Gyūnyū o nomu.
I drink milk.

Irui o gyū-gyū ni tsumekonda.
I squeezed all my clothes into the suitcase.

Gyoro-gyoro miru.
Look around wide-eyed.

Kanojo wa gyōgi ga warui.
She has bad manners.

NINE STROKES

Today's Target Kana For Stroke Practice

Last Kana			Next Kana
りょ	ぎゃ	ギャ	ぎゅ
RYO	Hiragana Soft Cursive Writing	Katakana Stiff Square Strokes	GYU

Hints For Stroke Order Reproduction And Recognition

(ぎゃ-**gya**), the pronunciation of this kana, is similar to the sound of this 'homemade word' "gi-yah." For the best stroke writing results, use a felt tip pen. Start from the left and follow the arrows. Using the very first kana as an example, slowly, with a light steady hand, try to accurately form your target kana. Use all the blank box spaces and imitate the strokes of your present and last kana until your kana resemble the original ones.

Target Strokes	1	2	3	4	5	6	7	8	9
ぎゃ									
ギャ									

Basic Kana (ぎゃ-Gya) To (ぎょ-Gyo) Stroke Order

SEVEN STROKES

Today's Target Kana For Stroke Practice

Last Kana	Hiragana Soft Cursive Writing	Katakana Stiff Square Strokes	Next Kana
ぎゃ	ぎゅ	ギュ	ぎょ
GYA			GYO

Hints For Stroke Order Reproduction And Recognition

(ぎゅ-**gyu**), the pronunciation of this kana, is similar to the sound of this 'homemade word' "gi-you." For the best stroke writing results, use a felt tip pen. Start from the left and follow the arrows. Using the very first kana as an example, slowly, with a light steady hand, try to accurately form your target kana. Use all the blank box spaces and imitate the strokes of your present and last kana until your kana resemble the original ones.

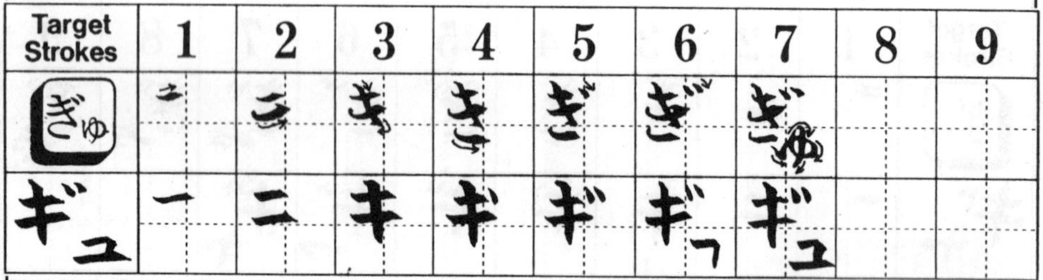

EIGHT STROKES

Today's Target Kana For Stroke Practice

Last Kana	Hiragana Soft Cursive Writing	Katakana Stiff Square Strokes	Next Kana
ぎゅ	ぎょ	ギョ	じゃ
GYU			JA

Hints For Stroke Order Reproduction And Recognition

(ぎょ-**gyo**), the pronunciation sound of this kana, is similar to the sound of this 'homemade word' "gi yo". For the best stroke writing results, use a felt tip pen. Start from the left and follow the arrows. Using the very first kana as an example, slowly, with a light steady hand, try to accurately form your target kana. Use all the blank box spaces and imitate the strokes of your present and last kana until your kana resemble the original ones.

Target Strokes	1	2	3	4	5	6	7	8	9
ぎょ									
ギョ	一	二	キ	ギ	ギ	ギ	ギョ	ギョ	

Basic Kana (ぎゃ-Gya) To (ぎょ-Gyo) Stroke Order

CREATIVE KANA REVIEW

Write it! Read it! Say it!

ぎゃ		ぎゅ		ぎょ
GYA		GYU		GYO

LINK-A-LETTER: You have already practiced writing all the hiragana on this page. Now use them to build new words in the adjoining boxes. Then try to link them to phrases.

ぎゃく **gyaku** reverse				ぎゅうにゅう **gyūnyū** milk			
ぎょうざ **gyōza** dumplings				ぎゅうにく **gyūniku** beef			
ぎゃくそう **gyakusō** return to sender				ぎゃくよう **gyakuyō** take advantage of			
ぎゃくせつ **gyakusetsu** paradox				ぎゅうじる **gyūjiru** one man rule			
ぎゃくしゅう **gyakushū** counter attack				ぎょうしゅく **gyoshuku** condense			

Make A Hiragana Word

THE IDEA ON HOW TO HANDLE THIS QUIZ APPEARED IN A SIMILAR QUIZ ON PAGE 245. USE THE WORDS YOU FORM TO MAKE SHORT PHRASES.

1 ______	4 ______	7 ______	10 ______
2 ______	5 ______	8 ______	11 ______
3 ______	6 ______	9 ______	12 ______

Vocabulary Expanding For Interacting
Using Imperatives

NATURAL SURVIVAL CONVERSATION

What You Might Hear	How You Might Possibly Answer
(O) **Kyō no yotei o yutte kudasai.** (E) Please tell me your agenda for today.	(O) **Kore ga kyō no yotei desu.** (E) This is it for today.
(O) **Wakiga dome o kudasai.** (E) Please give me some under-arm deodorant.	(O) **Mata waki no nioi o yuwareta no desu ka ?** (E) Were you criticized about your under-arm odor again ?
(P) **Massāji o shite kudasaimasen ka ?** (E) Can you please give me a massage ?	(O) **Honto ni shite hoshiin desu ka ?** (E) Are you sure you really want one ?
(O) **Watashi no kaban o watashite kudasai.** (E) Pass me my bag.	(O) **Doko ni arun desu ka ?** (E) Where is it ?
(O) **Shimbun o katte kite kudasai.** (E) Please go buy me a newspaper.	(O) **Nan no shimbun ga hoshiin desu ka ?** (E) What kind of newspaper do you want ?
(O) **Koko e motte kite kudasai.** (E) Please bring it here.	(O) **Motte kimashita.** (E) I brought it.
(C) **Are o chōdai.** (W) Give me that.	(O) **Kore dake de ii desu ka ?** (E) Is this all you want ?
(O) **Okane mo nai shi, chii mo nai sore ni, un mo nai.** (E) I have neither money, nor status nor luck.	(O) **Sore ja yosan no tsukaikata ni kiotsukenasai.** (E) Then you should keep tabs on your budget.
(O) **Kono pan o kitte kure.** (M) Cut this bread for me.	(O) **Naifu o kashite kudasai.** (E) Please lend me a knife.
(C) **Kore o kureru no ?** (E) Are you giving this to me ?	(C) **Kasu dake da yo !** (M) I'm only letting you borrow it.

Vocabulary Expanding For Interacting
Using Imperatives

NATURAL SURVIVAL CONVERSATION

What You Might Hear	How You Might Possibly Answer
(O) **Nanika tabemono o kuremasu ka?** (E) Can you let me have something to eat?	(O) **Kyō wa otetsudai-san no yasumi no hi desu.** (E) Today is the maid's day off.
(O) **Kore o chotto mite kure.** (M) Take a quick look at this.	(C) **Nanika machigai ga aru no?** (E) Are there any mistakes?
(C) **Kore o chotto mite goran.** (E) Try to take a brief look at this.	(C) **Mō mita yo!** (M) I've already seen it.
(O) **Taido o yoku shinakereba naranai.** (E) You have an attitude problem.	(O) **Kanpeki na hito wa itsumo hikan saremasu.** (E) Perfect people are always criticized.
(O) **Otoshi ga ikutsu daka wakarimasen ga chūnen no yō ni miemasu yo.** (E) I can't prove how old you are, but you seem to be middle-aged.	(O) **Atete goran, shikashi watashi wa funbetsu ga aru toshi de shikamo iron na koto ga kini naranai kurai wakai desu.** (M) Keep guessing but I'm old enough to know better and young enough not to care.
(O) **Tēburu no hata ni hata o okinasai.** (E) Place the flag close to the edge of the table.	(O) **Kantan da.** (M) That's easy to do.

Japanese FIGURE DESIGNATION

Imitate The Pronunciation And Duplicate The Writing

い ち	に	さ ん	し	ご
one	two	three	four	five
一	二	三	四	五
I	II	III	IV	V

256 Combined Kana Sound Changes Basic Kana (じゃ-Jya) To (じょ-Jyo) Stroke Order

Jaga-imo o fukasu.
Steamed potatoes.

Kare wa jumon o tonaeru.
He's murmuring a chant.

Juku ni kayou.
I go to prep school.

Jōdan iwanai de.
Don't joke!

Jōtō na okurimono.
It's a high quality gift.

SIX STROKES

Today's Target Kana For Stroke Practice

Last Kana	Hiragana Soft Cursive Writing	Katakana Stiff Square Strokes	Next Kana
ぎょ	じゃ	ジャ	じゅ
GYO			JYU

Hints For Stroke Order Reproduction And Recognition

(じゃ-**jya**) or (**ja**), the pronunciation of this kana, is similar to the first sound of the word "jazz". For the best stroke writing results, use a felt tip pen. Start from the left and follow the arrows. Using the very first kana as an example, slowly, with a light steady hand, try to accurately form your target kana. Use all the blank box spaces and imitate the strokes of your present and last kana until your kana resemble the original ones.

Target Strokes	1	2	3	4	5	6	7	8	9
じゃ	し	じ	じ	じっ	じゃ	じゃ			
ジャ	ヽ	ヽ	シ	ジ	ジ	ジァ	ジャ		

Basic Kana (じゃ-Jya) To (じょ-Jyo) Stroke Order

FOUR STROKES

Today's Target Kana For Stroke Practice

Last Kana	Hiragana Soft Cursive Writing	Katakana Stiff Square Strokes	Next Kana
じゃ	じゅ	ジュ	じょ
JYA			JYO

Hints For Stroke Order Reproduction And Recognition

(じゅ-**jyu**) or (**ju**), the pronunciation of this kana, is similar to the first sound of the word "juice." For the best stroke writing results, use a felt tip pen. Start from the left and follow the arrows. Using the very first kana as an example, slowly, with a light steady hand, try to accurately form your target kana. Use all the blank box spaces and imitate the strokes of your present and last kana until your kana resemble the original ones.

Target Strokes	1	2	3	4	5	6	7	8	9

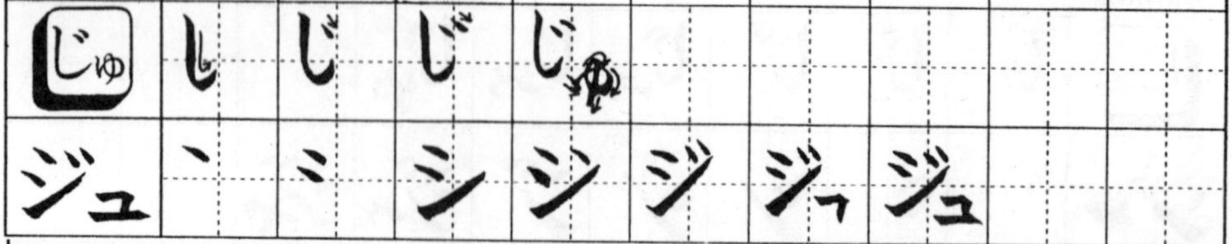

FIVE STROKES

Today's Target Kana For Stroke Practice

Last Kana	Hiragana Soft Cursive Writing	Katakana Stiff Square Strokes	Next Kana
じゅ	じょ	ジョ	びゃ
JYU			BYA

Hints For Stroke Order Reproduction And Recognition

(じょ-**Jyo**) or (**jo**), the pronunciation of this kana, is similar to the first sound of the word "joker." For the best stroke writing results, use a felt tip pen. Start from the left and follow the arrows. Using the very first kana as an example, slowly, with a light steady hand, try to accurately form your target kana. Use all the blank box spaces and imitate the strokes of your present and last kana until your kana resemble the original ones.

Target Strokes	1	2	3	4	5	6	7	8	9

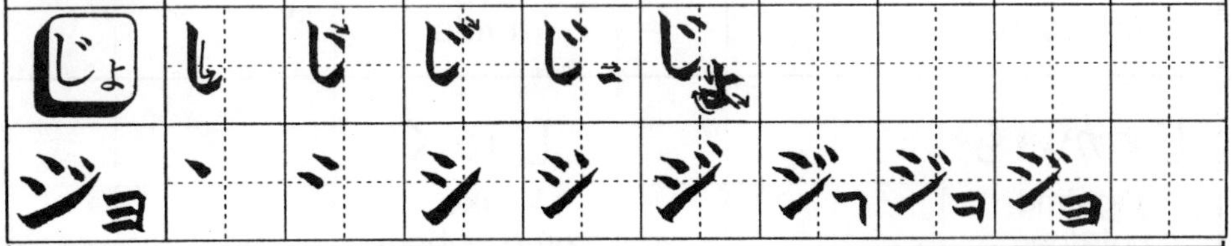

Basic Kana (じゃ-Jya) To (じょ-Jyo) Stroke Order

CREATIVE KANA REVIEW

Write it! Read it! Say it!

じゃ		じゅ		じょ
JYA		JYU		JYO

LINK-A-LETTER: You have already practiced writing all the hiragana on this page. Now use them to build new words in the adjoining boxes. Then try to link them to phrases.

じゅうぶん **jyūbun** just enough			じゃんけん **janken** hand game		
じょうず **jōzu** very good			じょうぎ **jōgi** a ruler		
じゃがいも **jagaimo** potatoes			じゅく **juku** prep school		
じょれつ **joretsu** grade, rank			じゅうどう **jūdō** martial art		
じゃり **jari** brat			じゃま **jama** to disturb someone		

IT'S NO SECRET ON HOW TO HANDLE THIS PAGE BECAUSE YOU'VE SEEN SIMILAR EXAMPLES ON TWO OTHER PAGES. MAKE FORMING WORDS IN HIRAGANA FUN. GOOD LUCK !

1 ______	4 ______	7 ______	10 ______
2 ______	5 ______	8 ______	11 ______
3 ______	6 ______	9 ______	12 ______

262

Vocabulary Expanding For Interacting

Natural Elements Plus Do (Suru) And Make (Naru)

NATURAL SURVIVAL CONVERSATION

What You Might Hear	How You Might Possibly Answer
(O) **Sensō wa takusan chi o nagasu. Heiwa wa chi ni hana o sakasu.** (E) War sheds a lot of blood while peace lets flowers bloom.	(O) **Minna shiawase ni naru.** (E) Everybody's gonna be happy.
(O) **Potsu-potsu to furu ame no oto wa suki desu.** (E) I love the sound of raindrops.	(P) **Issho ni amayadori o shimashō.** (E) Let's take shelter together from the rain.
(O) **Zā-zā to ōki na oto o tatete ame ga futte kita.** (E) The rain began coming down in torrents.	(O) **Isoide oitoma shimasu.** (E) We have to quickly hurry home.
(O) **Washi wa unga no ue o washi ga tobu no o mita.** (M) I saw an eagle fly over the canal.	(O) **Washi o tsukamae te miyō.** (E) I'd try to catch an eagle.
(O) **Bura bura to kōen o sanpo shita.** (E) I strolled around in the park.	(O) **Kibun ga ii yō na ki ga suru.** (E) I feel I'm in good health.
(O) **Chōchō ga chōchō to asonde iru.** (E) The mayor is playing with a butterfly.	(O) **Kare no taido wa ki ni naru.** (E) His attitude is making people anxious.
(O) **Konna ni shitsukoi ka ga anata no kinjo ni imasu ka?** (E) Are there many pesky mosquitos in your neighborhood?	(O) **Moshi itara satchū-zai o kake mashō.** (E) If there were I'd spray them.
(O) **Nomi wa chōkokushi no nomi ni tomatta.** (E) A flea sat on the sculptor's tool.	(O) **Muri o suru to nomi ni ikenaku naru.** (E) If he tries to do more than he can, then he can't go drinking.

Vocabulary Expanding For Interacting

Natural Elements Plus Do (Suru) And Make (Naru)

NATURAL SURVIVAL CONVERSATION

What You Might Hear	How You Might Possibly Answer
(O) **Sora ni wa ippen no <u>kumo</u> mo nai ga <u>kumo</u> ga oku o hashiri mawatte iru.** (E) Though there's no signs of <u>clouds</u> <u>spiders</u> are crawling around in the back.	(O) **Minna <u>kini suru</u>.** (E) Everyone's <u>anxious</u>.
(O) **<u>Zabu-zabu</u> to yogoreta <u>kawa</u> o <u>kawa</u> de aratta.** (E) I <u>vigorously</u> washed my dirty <u>leather</u> in the <u>river</u>.	(O) **Sappari to <u>kirei</u> ni natta.** (E) Now it's <u>clean</u>.
(O) **<u>Tsuki</u> no aru uchūhikōshi ga <u>tsuki</u> ni <u>tsuki</u> futatabi chikyū ni modotte kita.** (E) The <u>lucky</u> astronaut <u>landed</u> on the <u>moon</u> and returned to earth.	(O) **Subarashii <u>yō na kiga</u> suru.** (E) It seems like a <u>splendid feeling</u>.

Japanese FIGURE DESIGNATION

ろ く	し ち	は ち	く	じゅう
six	seven	eight	nine	ten
六	七	八	九	十
Ⅵ	Ⅶ	Ⅷ	Ⅸ	Ⅹ

じゅういち	じゅう に	じゅうさん
eleven	twelve	thirteen
十一	十二	十三

じゅう し	じゅう ご	じゅうろく
fourteen	fifteen	sixteen
十四	十五	十六

264 Combined Kana Sound Changes
Basic Kana (びゃ-Bya) To (びょ-Byo) Stroke Order

Byakuya da.
It's a white night.

Byū-byū kaze ga fuku.
The wind is blowing strongly.

Jidōsha ga byun-byun hashiru.
Cars are zooming by in the rush hour.

Byōki ga naotta.
I recovered from my illness.

SIX STROKES

Today's Target Kana For Stroke Practice

Last Kana			Next Kana
じょ	びゃ	ビャ	びゅ
JO	Hiragana Soft Cursive Writing	Katakana Stiff Square Strokes	BYU

Hints For Stroke Order Reproduction And Recognition

(びゃ-**bya**) is the pronunciation of this kana. It sounds like "be ya". For the best stroke writing results, use a felt tip pen. Start from the left and follow the arrows. Using the very first kana as an example, slowly, with a light steady hand, try to accurately form your target kana. Use all the blank box spaces and imitate the strokes of your present and last kana until your kana resemble the original ones.

Target Strokes	1	2	3	4	5	6	7	8	9

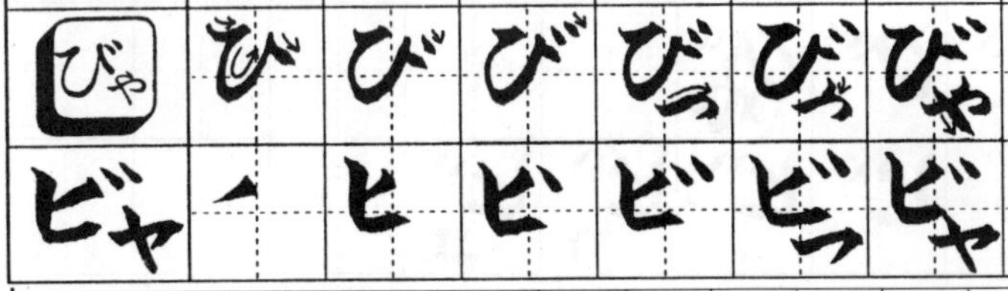

FOUR STROKES

Today's Target Kana For Stroke Practice

Last Kana	Hiragana Soft Cursive Writing	Katakana Stiff Square Strokes	Next Kana
びゃ	びゅ	ビュ	びょ
BYA			BYO

Hints For Stroke Order Reproduction And Recognition

(びゅ-byu) is the pronunciation of this kana. It sounds like "be you". For the best stroke writing results, use a felt tip pen. Start from the left and follow the arrows. Using the first kana as an example, slowly, with a light steady hand, try to accurately form your target kana. Use all the blank box spaces and imitate the strokes of your present and last kana until your kana resemble the original ones.

Target Strokes	1	2	3	4	5	6	7	8	9
びゅ	ひ	び	び	びゅ					
ビュ	ノ	ヒ	ビ	ビ	ビ	ビュ			

FIVE STROKES

Today's Target Kana For Stroke Practice

Last Kana	Hiragana	Katakana	Next Kana
びゅ	びょ	ビョ	ぴゃ
BYU	Hiragana Soft Cursive Writing	Katakana Stiff Square Strokes	PYA

Hints For Stroke Order Reproduction And Recognition

(びょ-byo) is the pronunciation of this kana. It sounds like "be yo". For the best stroke writing results, use a felt tip pen. Start from the left and follow the arrows. Using the very first kana as an example, slowly, with a light steady hand, try to accurately form your target kana. Use all the blank box spaces and imitate the strokes of your present and last kana until your kana resemble the original ones.

Target Strokes	1	2	3	4	5	6	7	8	9

Basic Kana (びゃ-Bya) To (びょ-Byo) Stroke Order

CREATIVE KANA REVIEW

Write it! Read it! Say it!

びゃ		びゅ		びょ
BYA		BYU		BYO

LINK-A-LETTER: You have already practiced writing all the hiragana on this page. Now use them to build new words in the adjoining boxes. Then try to link them to phrases.

びゃくだん **byakudan** sandalwood				びょうぶ **byōbu** folding screen			
さんびゃく **sanbyaku** three hundred				びゅうびゅう **byūbyū** sound of a strong wind			
びょういん **byōin** hospital				びょうき **byōki** sick			
びゃっこたい **byakko-tai** a historical hero				びょう **byō** seconds of clock time			
びゃっこ **byakko** a white fox				びゅう **byū** a zip sound			

SEARCH AND MATCH IDENTICAL KANA

Expand your kana recognition ability. Search within the numbers (1–5) for the kana which matches the left hand column Romanized letters. Write the correct kana in the blank boxes. Then use the bottom page boxes to practice any kana you wish.

Example :

Answer

			1	2	3	4	5
			↓	↓	↓	↓	↓
ga	←	3	だ	な	が	み	ぱ

Mark your correct answer numbers in these boxes below			1	2	3	4	5
		⬇	⬇	⬇	⬇	⬇	⬇
sa	⬅		き	る	さ	う	い
ko	⬅		に	こ	を	か	た
a	⬅		な	は	ほ	あ	う
ya	⬅		も	よ	く	や	ち
gu	⬅		ぐ	じ	づ	ぎ	げ

Practice writing any kana in these boxes

Vocabulary Expanding For Interacting
Identifying And Describing Yourself And Others

NATURAL SURVIVAL CONVERSATION

What You Might Hear	How You Might Possibly Answer
(C) **Kimitachi futari o dō yatte miwake yō ka?** (M) How can I tell you two apart?	(O) **Watashi wa iro-guro de sei ga hikuku kimbuchi no megane o kakete imasu. Tomodachi wa sei ga takaku irojiro de migi te ni shimbun o motte imasu.** (E) I'm earth-colored, short and wearing gold frame glasses. My friend is tall, piggy-pink and holding a newspaper in his right hand.
(O) **Bibi-kun no taijū to se no takasa wa dono kurai desu ka?** (E) What's Bibi's weight and height?	(O) **Hachijū-ni kiro de hyaku-nanajū senchi desu.** (E) He's 82 kilograms and 170 centimeters.
(O) **Toshi wa o-ikutsu desu ka?** (E) How old are you?	(P) **Kami-sama yori sansai ue desu.** (E) Three years older than God.
(C) **Atarashii rinjin ni atta ka?** (M) Did you meet our new neighbor?	(O) **Iie. Kare wa donna kakkō deshita ka?** (E) No. What did he look like?
(O) **Kare wa se ga hikuku, hara ga dete ite, akagede deppa de, mijikaku futoi ashi, kami o mannaka de wake, sanjū-dai no hito desu.** (E) He is short, pot-bellied, has red hair, buck teeth, short stubby legs, parts his hair in the middle and is thirtyish.	(O) **Kaibutsu eiga ni dete kuru hito o setsumei shite iru mitai desu ne.** (E) That sounds like you're describing some character in a freak movie.
(P) **Moshi, moshi, Gonkiberu-san no otaku desu ka?** (E) Hello, is this the Gonkibell's residence?	(O) **Hai, sō desu.** (E) Yes, it is.
(O) **Kōkoku no kaji-tetsudai ni ōbo shitain desu ga.** (E) I'd like to apply for the part-time home helper position you advertised.	(O) **Dōshite watashi no tokoro de hatarakitain desu ka?** (E) Why do you want to work for me?

NATURAL SURVIVAL CONVERSATION

What You Might Hear	How You Might Possibly Answer
(O) **Watashi ga saikin made tsutometa ie no shujin fūfu wa teroristo de hōkama de jibun no ie o moyashita hito deshita.** (E) The last couple I worked for turned out to be terrorists and arsonists who burned down their own home.	(P) **Anata ni kanshite sukoshi nanika oshiete kudasaimasen ka?** (E) Can you tell me a little about yourself?
(O) **Kami wa kuro de, hada wa hachimitsu no yōna iro de, itsumo niko-niko gao de, yasashii kanji no seikaku desu.** (E) I have black hair, a honey-colored complexion, a perpetually smiling face and pleasant personality.	(O) **Ashita no asa kuji kara hataraku tsumori naraba, sono toki, komakai koto o hanashi aimashō.** (E) If you're ready to start work at 9-am tomorrow, we can discuss the details then.

Japanese FIGURE DESIGNATION

じゅうしち seventeen 十七	じゅうはち eighteen 十八	じゅう く nineteen 十九
に じゅう twenty 二十	さんじゅう thirty 三十	よんじゅう forty 四十
ご じゅう fifty 50 五十	ひゃく hundred 100 百	せん thousand 1,000 千

272 Combined Kana Sound Changes
Basic Kana (ぴゃ-Pya) To (ぴょ-Pyo) Stroke Order

Kono kaidan wa roppyaku-dan desu.
This stairway has six hundred steps.

Pyū-pyū kuchi o narasu.
He's making a whistling sound.

Kaze ga tsuyoku pyū-pyū fukimasu.
The wind is blowing strongly.

Hiyoko ga pyoko-pyoko aruite iru.
The chicks are hopping about.

Watashi wa usagi ga pyon-pyon hanete nigeru oto o kiita.
I heard the rabbit hop quickly away.
*Pyon-pyon is a word used only in describing the sound of a rabbit and no other animal.

FIVE STROKES

Today's Target Kana For Stroke Practice

Last Kana	Hiragana Soft Cursive Writing	Katakana Stiff Square Strokes	Next Kana
びょ	ぴゃ	ピャ	ぴゅ
BYO			PYU

Hints For Stroke Order Reproduction And Recognition

(ぴゃ-**Pya**) is the pronunciation of this kana. It sounds like "pea ya". For the best stroke writing results, use a felt tip pen. Start from the left and follow the arrows. Using the very first kana as an example, slowly, with a light steady hand, try to accurately form your target kana. Use all the blank box spaces and imitate the strokes of your present and last kana until your kana resemble the original ones.

Target Strokes	1	2	3	4	5	6	7	8	9
ぴゃ	ひ	ぴ	ぴ	ぴ	ぴゃ				
ピャ	ノ	ヒ	ピ	ピ	ピャ				

Basic Kana (ぴゃ-Pya) To (ぴょ-Pyo) Stroke Order

THREE STROKES

Today's Target Kana For Stroke Practice

Last Kana	Hiragana Soft Cursive Writing	Katakana Stiff Square Strokes	Next Kana
ぴゃ	ぴゅ	ピュ	ぴょ
PYA			PYO

Hints For Stroke Order Reproduction And Recognition

(ぴゅ-**Pyu**) is the pronunciation of this kana. It sounds like "peau". For the best stroke writing results, use a felt tip pen. Start from the left and follow the arrows. Using the very first kana as an example, slowly, with a light steady hand, try to accurately form your target kana. Use all the blank box spaces and imitate the strokes of your present and last kana until your kana resemble the original ones.

Target Strokes	1	2	3	4	5	6	7	8	9
ぴゅ	び	ぴ	ぴゅ						
ピュ	ノ	ヒ	ピ	ピ	ピュ				

FOUR STROKES

Today's Target Kana For Stroke Practice

Last Kana: ぴゅ PYU

ぴょ ピョ

Hiragana Soft Cursive Writing

Katakana Stiff Square Strokes

Hints For Stroke Order Reproduction And Recognition

(ぴょ-**Pyo**) is the pronunciation of this kana. It sounds like "pea yo". For the best stroke writing results, use a felt tip pen. Start from the left and follow the arrows. Using the very first kana as an example, slowly, with a light steady hand, try to accurately form your target kana. Use all the blank box spaces and imitate the strokes of your present and last kana until your kana resemble the original ones.

Target Strokes	1	2	3	4	5	6	7	8	9
ぴょ	ひ	ぴ	ぴ	ぴょ					
ピョ	ノ	ヒ	ピ	ピ	ピョ	ピョ			

Basic Kana (ぴゃ-Pya) To (ぴょ-Pyo) Stroke Order

CREATIVE KANA REVIEW

Write it! Read it! Say it!

ぴゃ		ぴゅ		ぴょ
PYA		PYU		PYO

LINK-A-LETTER: You have already practiced writing all the hiragana on this page. Now use them to build new words in the adjoining boxes. Then try to link them to phrases.

いっぴょう **ippyō** one devotion				かんぴょう **kanpyō** ingredient of sushi			
はっぴょう **happyō** announcement				でんぴょう **denpyō** an office slip			
ぴゅうま **pyūma** a puma				ぴょこん **pyokon** to bobb one's head			
ぴゅうぴゅう **pyū pyū** to hiss				ぴょんぴょん **pyon pyon** to hop, skip and jump			
はっぴゃく **happyaku** eight hundred				ろっぴゃく **roppyaku** six hundred			

Try Translating These 12 Specific Occupations 277

See how quickly and accurately you can verbally translate these occupations into English. Then practice writing them into short phrases for phrase construction practice.

しょうぼうし	ごみしゅうしゅうにん	タクシーうんてんしゅ

けんせつさぎょういん	やねしょくにん	ディスクジョッキー

そうじゅうし	とこや	きじゅうきそうさしゃ

けいさつかん	かんごふ	だいく

278 Notes On Various Ways Of Counting

Of the many counter suffixes to be found in the Japanese language, those given on the next three pages are but a few of the more common ones you'll need to know to better understand the counting system. The counters shown in the paragraphs below do not appear with examples on other pages. They are presented as additional reference.

Japanese use the counter word **'kai'** to indicate the number of times they did something. **'Isseki'** is the counter word for one ship while **'ikki'** and **'niki'** are the counters for airplanes. One animal or fish gets counted as either **'hiki'** or **'biki'** but large animals are counted with **'hiki'** and **'tō.'** **'Jittō no uma'** means ten horses.

まい

Flat thin objects like sheets of paper, banknotes, postcards, compact discs, records, plates, sweaters, towels and even a slice of bread are counted with the counter '**mai**'.

Example :

(O) **Watashi ga neru toki futon ichi-mai zutsu basa-basa to shiku.**

(E) When I was about to go to sleep I noisily laid out futons one by one.

ほん

Thin long round objects like strands of hair, pencils, pens, cucumbers, and even chopsticks are counted by using either the counters '**pon**', **'bon,'** or **hon.'**

Example :

(O) **Chinbo no kami o puchi-puchi ippon ni-hon to nuitara tsuru-tsuru ni natta.**

(E) As I took out Chinbo's hair one by one his whole head became bald.

さつ

Flat objects like newspapers, books, magazines, and even calendars are counted by using the counter **'satsu.'** One calendar would also be counted as **'ichibu.'**

Example :

(O) **Issatsu no hon o biri-biri to yabuita.**

(E) I tore up one magazine bit by bit.

Notes On Various Ways Of Counting 279

だい

Large objects like various vehicles including cars, bicycles, motorcycles, machines, cardboard and wooden boxes are counted with the counter **'dai.'**

Example :

(O) **Ichi-dai no kuruma ga buku-buku to umi ni shizun-da.**

(E) One car sank into the ocean with a guzzling sound.

はこ

Anyother size box, regardless of number, gets counted with either the counters **'hako'** or **'bako.'**

Example :

(O) **Iro iro no macchi bako o motte ita ga bō-bō moete shimatta.**

(E) The various matchboxes I had went up in flames.

けん

Private homes get counted with the counter **'ken.'**

Example :

(O) **Yamaoku no ikkenya ni waza-waza tazunete itta.**

(E) I visited the house all the way up in the mountains.

にん

One human being gets counted as **'hitori'** and two as **'futari'.** From three people onwards they are counted with the counter '**nin**.' **San-nin** (three persons).

Example :

(O) **Jidai-geki no shujinkō ga basa-basa to nan nin mo kitta.**

(E) The hero in the samurai movie cut up a number of people swiftly.

さら

Any number of saucers or plates, even if they have something on them, get counted as **'sara.'**

Example :

(O) **Chūka ryōri de hito sara zutsu don-don tanonda.**

(E) At the Chinese restaurant we ordered a lot of one-plate food on and on.

280 Notes On various Ways of Counting

ひき

One animal or fish gets counted as **'biki'** or **'hiki.'**
Example :
(O) **Ippiki nezumi ga chū chū naite iru.**
(E) One mouse is making a crying noise.

こ

Any small object like stones, coins, light bulbs, buttons, ashtrays, small boxes of matches and even clothing pockets get counted with the counter **'ko.'**
Example :
(O) **Ikko niko to chiisai ishi o ikutsu mo ikutsu mo atsumeta.**
(E) I collected many a small pebble.

そく

'Soku' is the counter used for socks and shoes. **'Zoku'** is the counter for two or more.
Example :
(O) **Issoku no kutsushita o zutto haite itara boro-boro ni ana ga aita.**
(E) Since I wore one pair of socks for a long time they got shabby and developed holes.

Japanese FIGURE DESIGNATION

まん	じゅうまん	ひゃくまん
ten thousand	hundred thousand	million
10,000	100,000	1,000,000
万	十万	百万

せんまん	おく
ten million	hundred million
10,000,000	100,000,000
千万	億

1 ふたり

2 いっぴき

3 にまい

4 よんさつ

5 いっぽん

6 はちだい

7 いつつ

8 ふたやま

9 ひとさら

10 ひとはこ

11 いっさつ

12 いっけん

282 Japanese Numeral Counting Systems

Numbers Writing Practice

These two pages deal in number counting. Types of numbers are categorized according to the way they are used in referring to any number of items. For example '**sai**' refers to one's or someone else's age, whereas '**kono kai**' refers to 'this floor '. Try to write the Romanized numbers in hiragana. Practice pronouncing them and using them in phrases.

	Cardinal Number	**Things**	**Persons -nin**	**o'clock -ji**	**Floors -kai**	**Flat objects and lemons -mai**
1	ichi	hitotsu	hitori	ichi-ji	ik-kai	ichi-mai
2	ni	futatsu	futari	ni-ji	ni-kai	ni-mai
3	san	mittsu	san-nin	san-ji	san-gai	san-mai
4	shi yon	yottsu	yo-nin	yo-ji	yon-kai	yo(n)-mai
5	go	itsutsu	go-nin	go-ji	go-kai	go-mai
6	roku	muttsu	roku-nin	roku-ji	rok-kai	roku-mai
7	shichi nana	nanatsu	shichi-nin nana-nin	shichi-ji nana-ji	shichi-kai nana-kai	shichi-mai nana-mai
8	hachi	yattsu	hachi-nin	hachi-ji	hachi-kai hak-kai	hachi-mai
9	ku kyū	kokonotsu	ku-nin kyū-nin	ku-ji	kyū-kai	kyū-mai
10	jū	tō	jū-nin	jū-ji	jik-kai	jū-mai
11	jū-ichi	jū-ichi	jū-ichi-nin	jū-ichi-ji	jū-ik-kai	jū-ichi-mai
12	jū-ni	jū-ni	jū-ni-nin	jū-ni-ji	jū-ni-kai	jū-ni-mai
13	jū-san	jū-san	jū-san-nin		jū-san-gai	jū-san-mai
14	jū-shi jū-yon	jū-shi jū-yon	jū-yo-nin jū-yon-nin		jū-yon-kai	jū-yon-mai
15	jū-go	jū-go	jū-go-nin		jū-go-kai	jū-go-mai

16	jū-roku	jū-roku	jū-roku-nin		jū-rok-kai	jū-roku-mai
17	jū-shichi jū-nana	jū-shichi jū-nana	jū-shichi-nin jū-nana-nin		jū-shichi-kai jū-nana-kai	jū-shichi-mai jū-nana-mai
18	jū-hachi	jū-hachi	jū-hachi-nin		jū-hachi-kai jū-hak-kai	jū-hachi-mai
19	jū-ku jū-kyū	jū-ku jū-kyū	jū-ku-nin jū-kyu-nin		jū-kyū-kai	jū-kyū-mai jū-ku-mai
20	ni-jū	ni-jū	ni-jū-nin		ni-jik-kai	ni-jū-mai

	Banknotes, books, etc. -satsu	Round objects -hon	Cars and vehicles -dai	Notices in letter form -tsū
1	is-satsu	ip-pon	ichi-dai	it-tsū
2	ni-satsu	ni-hon	ni-dai	ni-tsū
3	san-satsu	san-bon	san-dai	san-tsū
4	yon-satsu	yon-hon shi-hon	yon-dai	yon-tsū
5	go-satsu	go-hon	go-dai	go-tsū
6	roku-satsu	rop-pon	roku-dai	roku-tsū
7	nana-satsu	shichi-hon nana-hon	shichi-dai nana-dai	nana-tsū
8	has-satsu	hachi-hon hap-pon	hachi-dai	hat-tsū
9	kyū-satsu	kyū-hon	kyū-dai	kyū-tsū
10	jis-satsu	jip-pon	jū-dai	jit-tsū

284 Try This Puzzle (Nazo Nazo)

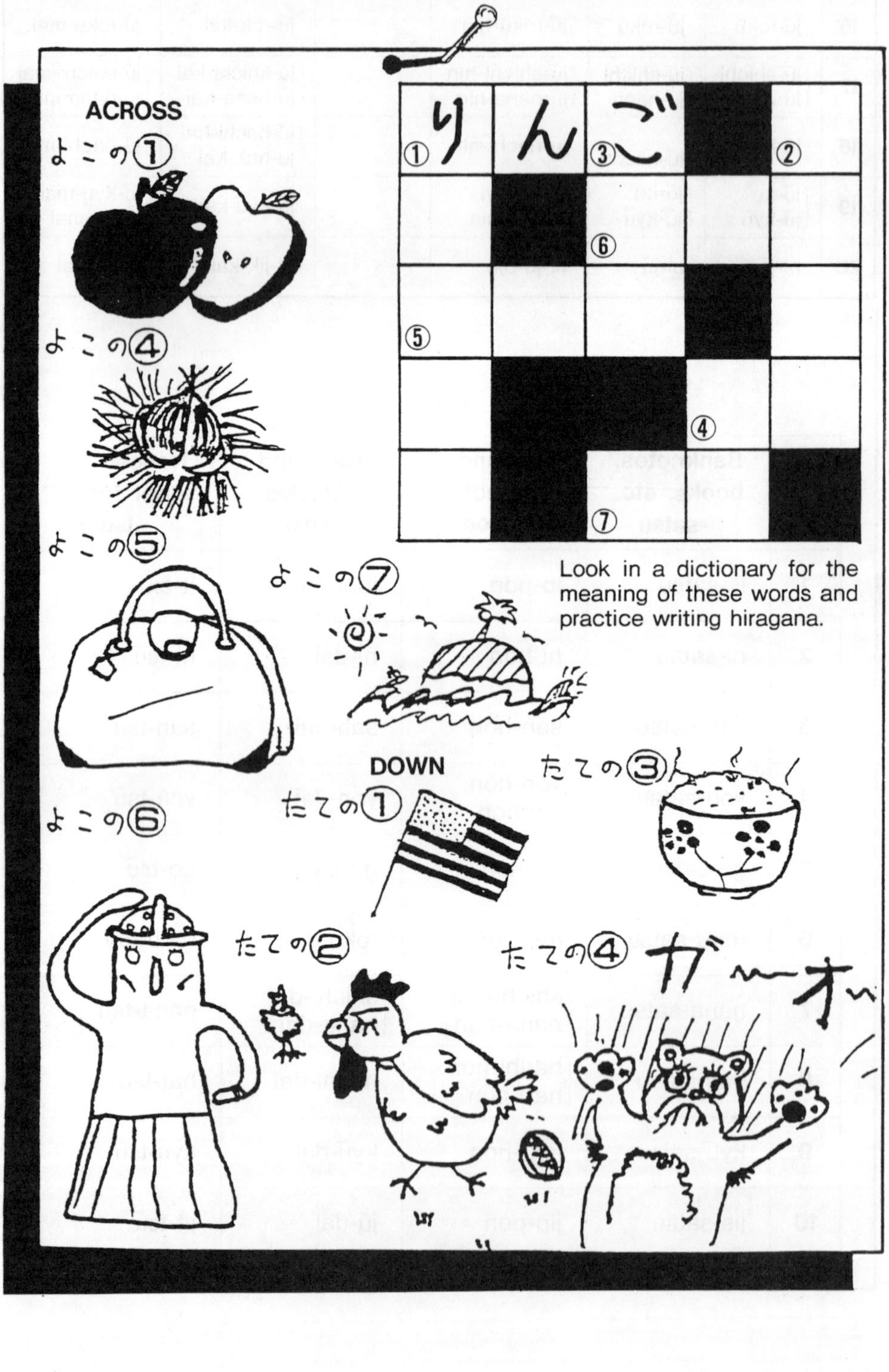

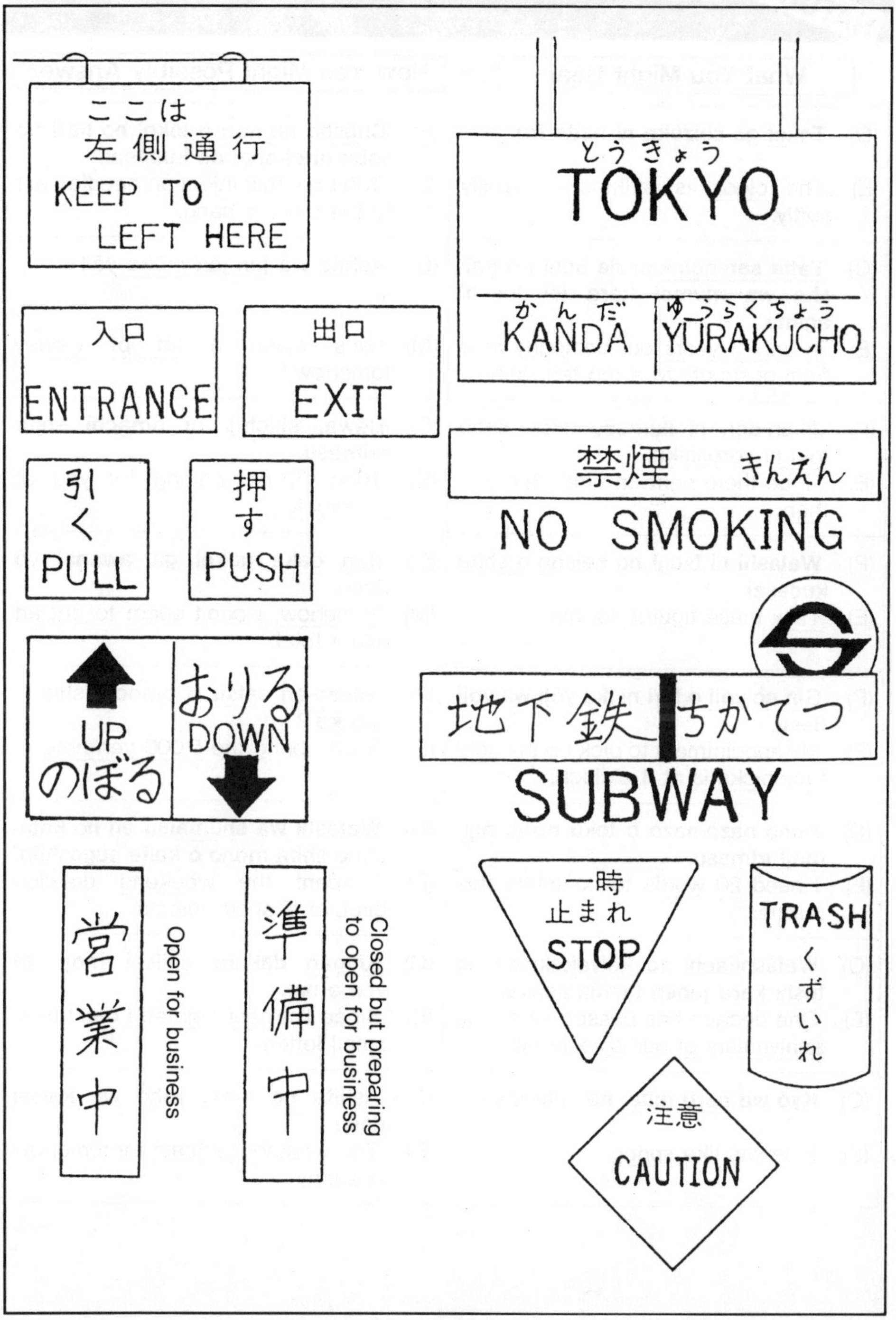
ここは
左側通行
KEEP TO
LEFT HERE
とうきょう
TOKYO
かんだ
KANDA
ゆうらくちょう
YURAKUCHO
入口
ENTRANCE
出口
EXIT
禁煙 きんえん
NO SMOKING
引く
PULL
押す
PUSH
UP
のぼる
おりる
DOWN
地下鉄 ちかてつ
SUBWAY
営業中
Open for business
準備中
Closed but preparing to open for business
一時
止まれ
STOP
TRASH
くずいれ
注意
CAUTION

Vocabulary Expanding For Interacting
Time, Numbers, Weather And Time of Day

NATURAL SURVIVAL CONVERSATION

What You Might Hear	How You Might Possibly Answer
(O) **Tokei ga shizuka ni natte iru.** (E) The clock is striking unusually softly.	(P) **Chūsha no hari o tokei no hari no soba ni okanai de kudasai.** (E) Don't put this injection needle next to the clock's hand.
(O) **Tatta san-nen-kan de uchi no kaisha wa mumei kara jōi jūi ni agatta.** (E) In only 3 years our company rose from obscurity to a top ten rating.	(C) **Ashita wa jan-jan mōke yō!** (M) Let's make a lot of money tomorrow!
(P) **Jikan-dōri ni ikimasu node sono toki ni yoroshiku.** (E) I'll be there right on time. See you then.	(P) **Dewa, shichiji ni omachi shite orimasu.** (E) Then I'll be waiting for you at 7 o'clock.
(P) **Watashi ni tsugi no keisan o shite kudasai.** (E) Tally these figures for me.	(O) **Nan daka gōkei ga awanai yō desu.** (M) Somehow, I can't seem to get an exact total.
(P) **Gin no yōji o tori ni iku yōji wa yoji desu.** (E) My appointment to pick up the gold toothpicks is at 4 o'clock.	(P) **Gosen-en satsu o omochi shimashō ka?** (E) Shall I bring the 5,000 yen note?
(O) **Kono nazo-nazo o toku no ni nijū moji irimasu.** (E) I need 20 words to complete this puzzle.	(O) **Watashi wa shūmatsu en no katachi o shita mono o kaite sugoshita.** (E) I spent the weekend drawing circular shaped objects.
(O) **Watashitachi no keiyakukinen no toshi kara jūnen tachimashita.** (E) One decade has passed since the anniversary of our agreement.	(O) **Kingan dakara chiisai moji ga yome nai.** (E) Since I'm near-sighted I can't read small letters.
(O) **Kyō wa haru mitai na yōki desu.** (E) It seems like spring.	(P) **Ashita no tenki yohō wa kaisei desu.** (E) The weather forecast for tomorrow is sunny.

NATURAL SURVIVAL CONVERSATION

What You Might Hear	How You Might Possibly Answer
(O) **Mō sugu fuyu ni narimasu ga. Hiruma yori yoru no hō ga nagaku narimasu.** (E) As winter approaches, the nights are longer than the days.	(O) **Dare demo fuyu wa buru-buru fu-rueru deshō.** (E) Anyone would shiver in the winter.
(O) **Watashi wa yoru anata no ie ni yoru.** (E) I will drop by your home at night.	(C) **Watashi no ie ni yoru osoku choku-choku asobi ni kuru.** (E) He often visits my home late at night.
(O) **Watashitachi wa shitashiku kuchi o kikanai.** (E) We are not on good speaking terms.	(P) **Sonna koto wa dō demo iin desu.** (E) It doesn't really matter.
(O) **Ima kara sōji o suru.** (E) I'm going to clean the house now.	(O) **Dōzo, o-saki ni.** (E) Please, go ahead.
(O) **Tō no tō wa tō de atsumari-masen.** (E) Ten political parties can't meet in the tower.	(O) **Gizen teki na seijika wa kyokutan na atsukamashisa to shinsetsusa o sonaete iru.** (E) Hypocritical politicians are full of extreme rudeness and politeness.

Japanese FIGURE DESIGNATION

WESTERN	0	½	1	2	3	4	5	6	7	8	9	10	100
BURMESE	၀	[illegible]	၁	၂	၃	၄	၅	၆	၇	၈	၉	၁၀	၁၀၀
THAI・LAOS	๐	[illegible]	๑	๒	๓	๔	๕	๖	๗	๘	๙	๑๐	๑๐๐
JAPANESE		半	一	二	三	四	五	六	七	八	九	十	百
OFFICIAL CHINESE	零	半	壹	貳	叁	肆	伍	陸	柒	捌	玖	拾	佰
COMMERCIAL CHINESE			〡	〢	〣	〤	〥	〦	〧	〨	〩	十	
KOREAN		반	일	이	삼	사	오	육	칠	팔	구	십	백
ETHIOPIAN	◆		፩	፪	፫	፬	፭	፮	፯	፰	፱	፲	፻

288 First Steps To Actually Writing Hiragana

Since you already know the basic hiragana stroke writing order, you should now feel confident enough to venture into writing phrases and whole sentences. But first, you are strongly advised to review hints given on **Basic Steps To Forming Japanese Sentences**, particles, and **Three Ways To Finish Writing A Stroke**.

A point of advice to keep in mind ; a lot of the Japanese being taught outside Japan is not actually spoken by the Japanese. For few people use such sanitized phrases and polite terms of speech except in special cases. Most of their daily social conversation is naturally learned as a tot at their mother's knee ; this is what will be found in conversation sections of this book. It's not the bookish style mainly taught. Thus it would be to your benefit, in order to better recognize what is said to you, that you come up with an appropriate potential response by going over the Romanized conversation sections of this book.

Even with a fair command of the Japanese language and its grammar, it's hard to master the Japanese way of thinking. In fact, five Japanese could be given an English sentence to translate into Japanese and seldom will they all come up with a unified translated version. And this holds true for translating all the Romanized sentences found in this book. So don't feel too bad when you have difficulty in communicating with the Japanese. Just don't give up too easily.

Sentence Punctuation Tips

。← Called *'kuten'* this symbol is the Japanese equivalent to an English period except that it is a circle (*maru*) and not a black dot. Still, it always goes at the end of a sentence.

、← Called *'toten'* this symbol is the Japanese equivalent to an English comma and is called a dot (*ten*). Nowadays, however, the real English comma is used when writing Japanese horizontally.

「」﹁﹂← Called *'kagi-kakko'* these two types of brackets are used as Japanese quotation marks to quote remarks made by one or more persons. This → 「」 you'd use when writing horizontally and this →﹁﹂ when writing vertically. Notice their shapes carefully.

Although when writing in formal correspondence one would not use exclamation or question marks, they are used without restriction in informal letters and even novels.

Now we get into the actual scheme of things. Take a good look at the horizontal and vertical model phrases and sentences, paying special attention to the position of each punctuation mark.

(Start from left)

Kagikakko (Brackets) and Kuten (Period)

「ふといですね。」

This is thick.

Contracted Sound

「かれはびょうきです。」

He's sick.

(Writing vertically from right)

ばったり

By chance.

「おてあらいは、どこですか。」

Where is the public restroom ?

ひょうきんなかのじょ

She's comical.

あのひと
たちは、
どこから
きましたか。

Where are they from ?

おいしい
かな。

I wonder if it's delicious.

みょうじは、
いとう

My surname is Ito.

これだけ
です。

This is all.

Writing Horizontally (Comma)

そうですが、

But...

Writing Vertically

でんぽうがあった

I received a telegram.

Voiced Syllable

Period

さむいです。

It's cold.

いやだ

I don't like it.

Contracted Sound

びょうきです。

I'm sick.

BRIEF PARTICLE FLASHBACK REVIEW

Every particle has several usages, as you can notice by some of the examples given. Many non-Japanese find particles difficult to use in conversation. But with much practice their usage will eventually become second nature in your speech patterns. When in doubt, ask if you're right and ask to be corrected. Now, let's review just a few particles which you have already read about.

(は-**wa**) It indicates a sentence's topic or subject.
Kanojo wa kare ni kin-en saseta.
She made him stop smoking.

(か-**ka**) It is always placed at the end of any sentences you wish to turn into a question.
Itsu mata ae masu ka ? (or, **o-ai deki masu ka ?**)
When can we meet again?

(の-**no**) It follows a noun which is modifying another noun.
Tabako no kemuri ga kirai desu.
I dislike tobacco smoke.

(も-**mo**) It can be translated into English to mean either 'too', 'as well', or 'also'.
Sensei mo kaomake.
She put the teacher to shame.
Mitto mo nai bideo sae nai.
I don't even have a video.

(に-**ni**) It may be used to express three different positions: 'to indicate the time of day an action took place', 'an indirect object', and 'to express the location where something is.'
(O) **Watashi no kazoku wa gose-dai mae kara kono kuni ni imasu.**
(E) My family's been in this country since five generations ago.

(O) **Asa ni asa no fuku o mitsukerarenai.**
(E) In the morning I couldn't find my linen clothes.

(を-**o**) It indicates a direct object.
(O) **Ano fuku ga tsuiteru hito ni fuku o agenasai.**
(E) Give clothes to that lucky man.

(P) **Dōzo kono zōteiken o uketotte kudasai.**
(E) Please accept this gift certificate.

(え-**e**) It specifies the noun indicating direction used with verbs of motion such as 'come,' 'go' and 'return.'

(O) **Shigatsu ni Tokyo e kaerimashita.**
(E) I returned to Tokyo in April.

(P) **Roma e itsu otachi desu ka?**
(E) When are you going to leave for Rome?

(で-**de**) There are various ways of using this particle. For example 'means of transportation' or of doing something.

(O) **Atta ue de hanashimasu.**
(E) I'll talk about it when we meet.

(と-**to**) It occurs between two connecting nouns.

(O) **Takarakuji ga ataru to ureshii.**
(E) If I win a lottery I'll be happy.

*Further Notes On The Workings Of Particles

The all-important role particles perform in Japanese sentences can't be stressed enough. Notice these four examples.

1) (O) **Kare ga sappari wakaranai.**
(E) He doesn't understand it at all.
*__Kare__ is the subject when **ga** is present.

2) (O) **Kare o sappari wakaranai.**
(E) I don't understand him at all.
*__Kare__ is the object when **o** is present.

3) (O) **Kare niwa ageru.**
(E) I'll give it only to him.

4) (O) **Kare nimo ageru.**
(E) I'll give it to him, too.

* In short, particles stress the exact relationship between words. If you were to say '**watashi wa**' that means you're talking only about yourself and no one else. Without a particle a sentence would be lopsided. Do remember this.

294 Anatomy Language Writing Practice

The hiragana placed under each letter gives you a Japanese translation of that word as well as an opportunity to see it written. Try reading and pronouncing each word aloud just in case of an emergency.

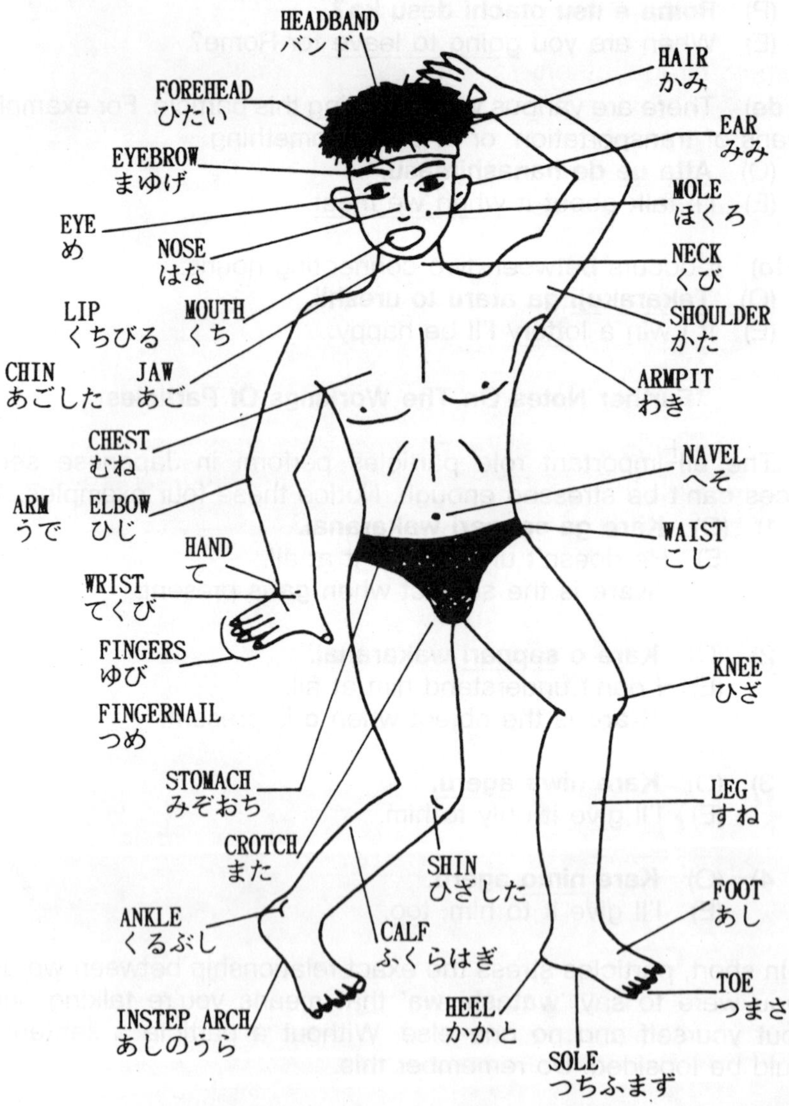

Hiragana Sentence Completion Practice

Do your best to complete each sentence by filling in each space with the proper missing hiragana ideogram. After that transcribe each sentence into Romaji. Have your strokes checked for accuracy in shape and size.

Example hiragana sentence to practice writing
(Write the missing letters in the boxes)
うでをおった。
I broke my arm.

う				っ		。

Now, write the Romaji for this sentence.

This example is a complete sentence. Write the missing hiragana ideographs in their correct boxes below and read them aloud.

か	み	の	け	が
て	か	て	か	。

Write all the missing letters in the blank boxes you see, like this one. Start from the left.

	み			が
				。

296 12 Animals Of The Oriental Zodiac (Horoscope)

Tokyo Traveler's English

TELEPHONE

Bulletin Board INFORMATION

* The numbers in parenthesis are area code numbers. For example since (03) is for the Tokyo area, it is not necessary to dial '3' within Tokyo.

Police ☎ 110
Tokyo Immigration Office ☎ 213-8111
International Telephone Calls ☎ 0051(for operator assistance)
English Telephone Service ☎ 201-1010 (10-am to 7-pm weekdays)
Yokohama English Telephone ☎(045) 322-1010
Narita English Telephone ☎(0476) 28-1010
Japan Hotline ☎ 586-0110(Mon-Fri 10-am to 4-pm)
24-hour Japan Helpline ☎ 0120-461-997
English Weather Report ☎(0476) 28-8899
American Embassy ☎ 224-5000
Canadian Embassy ☎ 408-2101
West German Embassy ☎ 473-0151
French Embassy ☎ 473-0171
Taxi Lost Property ☎ 355-0300
American Pharmacy ☎ 271-4034(Tokyo) ☎(078) 262-2577(Kobe)
(American and European medicines … English speaking staff.)
Hibiya Park Bldg. (Open 9-am to 7-pm) (open 7 days a week)
Tourist Information Center ☎ 502-1461
Toppan Travel Service ☎ 276-8101
(Philip Gzell, President, friendly and helpful)
G.T.L. Ganymedes Tours Ltd.
P.O. Box 30477, 100 33 Athens, Greece ☎ 721-4821
(Office also in Chicago, President George Soultis very friendly and helpful) ☎ 800-621-9216 (U.S.A)
Ryuseido Drug Store
(discount chain throughout Tokyo, especially underground Shinjuku Station)
Attorney Yu Sato ☎ 502-5467
He's very sincere, helpful and speaks some English.
Foreign Advisory Service ☎ 211-4433
Their English-speaking staff will help to solve your problems as best they can. (9:30-12 and 1-4)
Hiragana Times, Mr. Nomura, Editor ☎ 341-8989
The only tabloid in Japan printed in Hiragana and English.

A Brief Biogra-file On Your Author

Genuine native New Yorker, 'Michael', as Mike Hooser is addressed by his intimate friends, is a graduate of Tokyo's prestigious Waseda University and holder of a teacher's license issued from the Japanese Ministry of Education via its Faculty of Education. At their campus as well as at Osaka University of Foreign Studies and Columbia University in New York, is where he studied Japanese.

A resident of over 12 years in Tokyo, Michael has traveled extensively throughout Southeast Asia. His 17 books have varied from English as a second language manuals for Japanese wanting to brush up their English, Japanese conversation books (2) for non-Japanese speakers, and travel guidebooks dealing mainly with Asia. Some of his more recognized books include Japan Airline's very first original English language guidebook on the People's Republic of China, the timely Jet-Setters' Guide To Korea for the Seoul 1988 Summer Olympics, and books on Thailand and the Philippines.

Because of the two Japanese conversation books he's written ('Japan Bound Visitors' Japanese Conversation is available from : Yohan Pub Tokyo, Tel : 03-208-0181 ; 'Jet-Age Japanese' is out of publication), Michael felt it was about time he came up with one for writing the language as well and this book is representative of the time and effort he devotes to his books on behalf of his loyal readers. In 1984 Michael produced the world's very first reversable, bilingual (English/Japanese), illustrated phrase-a-day wall calendar, simultaneously copyrighted in Canada and America. There's no telling what this versatile author will do next, but no doubt he'll give it his best creative effort. He's always receptive to his readers' needs, ideas and suggestions and welcomes their letters addressed to him at : P. O. Box 139, Shinjuku, Tokyo 163-91, Japan.

SCRATCH N' MIMIC HIRAGANA
ひらがな百科

1990年7月10日　初版発行

著　者　マイク・フーザー
発行者　株式会社 北星堂書店
代表者　山本雅三
〒113 東京都文京区本駒込3-32-4
Tel (03) 827-0511　Fax (03) 827-0567

検印省略

THE HOKUSEIDO PRESS
32-4, Honkomagome 3-chome, Bunkyo-ku, Tokyo 113 Japan

定価 2800円 (本体 2718円)